PLAY IT
to WIN

STRATEGIES FOR MILLENNIALS STARTING
IN CORPORATE AMERICA

NEFRETITI NASSAR

For more information or requests for speaking
engagements, contact:

Nefretiti Nassar

info@nefretitinassar.com

www.nefretitinassar.com

ISBN 978-1-7329655-0-8

Printed in the United States of America

10 9 8 7 6 5 4 3 2 1

For the generation now and others to come,

may this book inspire strategic thinking

for you to become who you were created to be.

Contents

Part Three
Strategic Planning

Part Four
Strategic Development

Foreword

One of the greatest lessons in life is self-discovery. I never knew how strategic I am until I was faced with the challenges and struggles I found in Corporate America. The process of overcoming them necessitated a diverse set of strategies that has helped evolve me into the professional woman I am today, a technical leader and growing manager in the field of engineering.

Play It to Win: Strategies for Millennials Starting in Corporate America was written to help Millennials to successfully navigate the workplace and its politics by equipping them with strategies to increase their performance, image, and exposure, which collectively lead to a successful career. This book is a compilation of strategies to help support Millennials as they pursue their aspirations.

Introduction

Navigating the workplace is not an easy feat. In fact, it's more complicated than most of us can imagine. The challenges of navigating politics in the workplace and learning the unwritten rules can be overwhelming, exhausting, and stressful. Learning what not to do, what to do, and when to do it isn't always straightforward. Your idea of how people in the workplace perceive you can also be misleading. Even knowing these challenges, avoiding workplace politics is impossible.

Play It to Win: Strategies for Millennials Starting in Corporate America is a supplementary resource to help minimize the trial and error incurred when transitioning into Corporate America or starting a new job there. It provides you with guidance, practical examples, strategic advice, and words of wisdom in the form of "*Nefisms*" to increase your chances of successfully navigating many unwritten rules within the workplace.

Part One

Fundamental Strategies

Build a solid foundation to establish your career.

1

Establish Your Performance

Your performance in the workplace lays the foundation for your success in the chess game of Corporate America. Without strong and solid performance, you will find it increasingly difficult to develop the credibility you'll need to excel. You see that credibility earned in the workplace is largely built upon your ability to solve problems and deliver solutions on time. Both are tied to your performance. So as you start your career in Corporate America as a full-time professional employee, be mindful that people are most likely unfamiliar with your ability to execute plans and solve problems. They just haven't witnessed how awesome you are yet. Therefore, starting on your first day, begin building your credibility as an employee through your performance and in due season, everyone will see just how great you are.

When given a task or assignment to perform, ensure you have the following information:

- A clear understanding of the problem you are being asked to solve
- An awareness of the boundaries and constraints associated with the problem space
- What is expected as a deliverable
- When the task or assignment is due
- If applicable, an example of previous or similar deliverables

Your ability to solve problems in the workplace necessitates a clear understanding of the problems you are being asked to solve. The key is to ask questions for clarification. When you fully understand what you are being asked to do, you increase the probability of being able to solve the problem which can positively influence your performance.

Most problems given to you to solve have inherent boundaries and constraints associated with them. Gaining an awareness of these boundaries and constraints will positively influence your performance—this is where playing it to win comes into play. Most people starting in the workplace do not consider boundaries and constraints when problem-solving. However, if you ask questions to identify the true problem parameters, you will have the advantage of solving the specific problem at hand, the first time, and perhaps before the scheduled deadline. It also allows you to focus your skills and knowledge to perform most efficiently.

Before you begin solving a problem assigned to you, you must know what is expected as a deliverable. Ask your task lead, "What type of format are you looking for?" You can also suggest formats in which you can deliver the solution. By offering a suggested format or agreeing upon one, you influence how the solution will be delivered. This is playing it to win because you're influencing the deliverable into a format that you are already knowledgeable or skilled at, thus increasing your ability to perform at an optimum level.

Once you fully understand the task or problem, you need to ask when the task or assignment is due. It's critical that your task lead and you concur on a deadline. Your ability to deliver a solution within the given time constraint will demonstrate your performance level and help you build your credibility with that person.

Asking to see an example of previous or similar deliverables can contribute to your performance level. Examples provide you with insight into how your lead, organization, or company typically deliver solutions. Playing it to win is about being strategic in your approach, so intel on how the business currently delivers solutions will help you tailor your problem-solving approach and increase your awareness of your needed level of performance.

In the workplace, your performance will be assessed against that of your peers. Knowing this, you should perform at a level above your counterparts to gain recognition that will distinguish you—this is how you play it to win. But how do you do this? By becoming a high-performing employee.

Become a High-Performing Employee

A high-performing employee is an individual who continuously exceeds the level of expectations assigned to him or her. They are exceptional and you will know them when you meet them. Some say that high-performing employees are generally driven and solution-oriented. I've noticed that they tend to focus on delivering high-quality solutions beyond the minimum requirements. But these are only some of the characteristics of those we arguably call high performers. Nonetheless, if you're going to play the chess game of Corporate America, you must become a high-performing employee to win in the workplace.

How I Began Establishing Myself as a High-Performing Employee

I joined a Fortune 500 company after my college graduation. For the first three to four months of employment, I spent time learning about the program work I was designated to do. During this time, I also observed the team I was working with to help develop and deliver solutions for the customer. As individuals on the team provided weekly status updates on daily tasks, I gained an understanding of the level of performance our task lead expected. Shortly after, I began going above the average expectation by delivering solutions before the anticipated deadline, suggesting next steps for moving forward, researching information about our subject area and sharing it with the team, and offering to help other team members complete their tasks. Performing such tasks immediately distinguished me as a valuable member of the team. As a result of actively demonstrating high performance and providing valuable contributions to the team, our task lead started to increase my level of responsibilities by providing me opportunities to demonstrate my knowledge, skills, and level of performance beyond the boundaries of just our team. This was the beginning of developing my brand within the company as a high-performing employee.

Strategies to become a high-performing employee:

- Develop quality solutions and demonstrate knowledge and proficiency.
- Consistently deliver solutions ahead of schedule.
- Offer alternative solutions or approaches to help solve problems.
- Bring solutions, not problems, to leadership.
- Leverage lessons learned from previous projects to increase efficiency.
- Share best practices to increase productivity.
- Extend yourself and your time to help others solve their problems.

High-performing employees develop quality solutions that exceed expectations. These employees strive to create solutions that will not only satisfy the customer but also provide maximum impact—that's how you play it to win. A maximum impact could include: providing an executive summary, incorporating an analysis of alternatives, identifying potential risks, supplementing the solution with a detailed analysis, adding illustrations to the solution, etc. These are ways you can demonstrate your knowledge and proficiency and set yourself apart from your counterparts. Further, high-performing employees understand that a satisfied customer will typically request their services again in the future, meaning if you satisfy your task lead, he or she will likely offer you additional opportunities to perform and exhibit your capability to solve problems, thus increasing your credibility within the workplace.

High-performing employees consistently deliver solutions ahead of schedule. They recognize that delivering a solution before the deadline will set them apart from their colleagues. This ability to deliver solutions ahead of schedule is also a reflection of the employee's drive and ambition. It is these qualities that shape the performance of a high-performing employee, attract people to want to work with them, and expand their opportunities to perform across different platforms and avenues.

Offering alternative solutions or approaches to solving problems will contribute to your capability as a high-performing employee. Organizations have varying levels of complex problems that need to be solved. Generally, people within a workplace develop a regimen of approaching and solving problems that aligns with their usual way of business. However, if you can think outside the box and offer alternative solutions or approaches that can positively impact the business and the delivery of a solution, you will excel—and this is where playing it to win comes into play. By positioning yourself as a strategist within your current role, you become a resource whom people in the workplace consult. As more people seek your counsel, you increase your influence within your organization and even across the overall company, which is the ultimate strategic move.

Leadership within an organization and across a company consistently face problems. High-performing employees acknowledge the pressures placed on leadership and bring them solutions, not problems. Managers already have enough fires to put out, so adding fuel to the fire does not help them. If you become an employee who can solve and mitigate problems independently, you will be praised for your ability to get the job done. Leadership likes results, not problems, so through your performance, build the reputation of being able to deliver with minimum supervision. These are the types of people whom company leaders prefer to work with.

Leveraging lessons learned from previous projects can help increase your performance efficiency. These lessons learned give insight into what worked well and what didn't for a comparable project. They help you tailor your approach to a problem, reducing or even eliminating issues that could potentially occur in your development of a solution. High-performing employees leverage their own lessons learned or seek them from others to maximize their performance and deliver quality solutions.

Sharing best practices tends to increase productivity. It creates alignment or commonality of application across multiple organizations. Your ability to compile recommended industry standards, share them with your team, and apply them to problems displays your initiative and commitment to developing quality solutions. It also shows your ability to stay abreast of industry trends in an effort to remain relevant and current on the topic at hand—this is playing it to win because it helps increase your relevance and influence within your domain and workplace organization.

Extending yourself and time to help others in the workplace is admirable and will serve you well in your endeavors. We all need help sometimes, no matter where we sit within the hierarchy of the organization. Becoming a resource for others by extending your time, resources, and influence is a great service in the workplace, regardless of its size. Demonstrating this ability to lend a helping hand, especially when it is most needed, will positively shape how people view you and will yield greater credibility. As a high-performing employee, offer your time to help others solve their individual problems; this will help set you apart.

Your performance within the workplace influences the type of opportunities that will be afforded to you. Those who are high performers and have developed a level of credibility are usually tasked with more challenging problems to solve, outweighing the mundane tasks that just need to get done or assignments that require minimal effort or skill. You can identify how others perceive your professional performance by the type of work you are assigned and privileged to do, or the problems and concerns you are trusted to know about and contribute to solving.

Perform at the Next Level

Whenever you're interested in getting promoted to the next level, you should begin performing at that next level, while still at your current level. Identify the roles and responsibilities recommended at the next level and begin to demonstrate them in your current role. By doing so, you express your capability to perform and execute beyond the boundaries of your current placement, thus qualifying you as a candidate for promotion.

My Approach for Performing at the Next Level

Every eighteen months, I believe an employee should take on a new opportunity that challenges him or her to develop a new skill or mature an existing skill. After working for eighteen months at the company, I was presented a new opportunity to apply my skills and knowledge to a different subject area and organization within the company. I quickly gained an understanding of the need I was being asked to fill, and then I began solving problems and asking questions whenever I needed clarification on a task or a greater understanding of the problem. Shortly after that, I was paired with an employee at my direct next level for job shadowing. Job shadowing is following someone as they're doing their day-to-day tasks to gain a greater understanding of how to do specific work activities. I did job shadowing for four to six months; it was a valuable platform that helped prepare me for the next level. When it was time to set performance goals for the next year, I communicated to my manager that I was interested in being promoted, and I asked what I needed to do to advance to the next level. That conversation led to a review of the performance expectations for the next level and for the upcoming year. I performed at the next level while still in my current position, and the following year, I was promoted.

Strategies to get your performance ready for the next level:

- Communicate your interest to perform at the next level.
- Seek new opportunities that will allow you to showcase your performance capability at the next level.
- Observe the performance of others at the next level.
- Be willing to learn new things.
- Collaborate with others at the next level to solve complex problems.

When you're interested in being promoted, first communicate this interest to your direct manager, making him or her aware of your desire to assume a position at the next level. Discuss what's required to get there and how you should begin performing to gain that promotion.

A promotion usually requires an opportunity to showcase your performance capability at the next level. Therefore, seek ways to expand your current role and responsibilities on your current project or seek new opportunities that will increase your responsibilities and allow you to perform at the next level. You need an opportunity that will provide you the necessary structure to acquire new knowledge, mature your current skill set, and develop the needed skill sets for your next role. The ultimate goal is depth and breadth of knowledge and experience—that's positioning yourself to play it to win!

When considering a move to the next level, observe the performance of others already at that level. Watch how they conduct business, approach problems, deliver solutions, etc. Their actions and interactions reflect how the organization expects people at that particular level to operate. Use them as a reference point at your own discretion. It will serve you well to examine the performance of others at your desired level of promotion so you can adjust your current performance accordingly.

A great way to prepare your performance for the next level is by being open to learning new things. This by far is the best way to seek new opportunities that can provide you the platform to further develop and expand your skills and experiences. Being willing to learn new things allows you to explore new areas of development while expanding your performance across diverse organizations within your company—this is playing it to win! It allows you to strategically expand your credibility and influence throughout the company.

Collaborating with others at the next level to solve complex problems is a direct way to prepare your performance for advancement. This collaboration will allow you to witness the type of effort that is needed to solve problems at their level. You gain a better understanding of the types of problems they face, the approaches they can explore, and the available resources at their disposal to solve problems. Additionally, you can gain insight into how they balance the demands of their role and responsibilities. Collaborating with others at the next level truly provides you with an opportunity to shadow someone in a role you aspire to assume. This is beneficial to your development because it helps you to refine your interests within your organization and across the company.

Prioritizing Work Assignments

Learning to prioritize your work can complement the proficiency of your performance. Prioritization necessitates time management and organization. To be effective and efficient, you need to allocate your performance availability, which many in the workplace describe as bandwidth. Understanding your bandwidth and capacity to take on additional work will help you focus on problems for which you can deliver quality solutions. Remember, the fundamental goal is earning credibility through performance, so you want to strive to influence situations that will increase the probability of delivering quality solutions on time or ahead of time, if possible.

How I Prioritize Work to Help
Ensure My Success

In college, as an undergraduate engineering student, I learned that time management and work prioritization were critical to balance a full-time schedule and leadership roles in professional societies. I carried this lesson into the workplace, and it served me well. While at work, I learned over time, the rate at which I could complete tasks of varying levels of difficulty. This helped me to develop an understanding of my personal bandwidth. So when my task lead or manager asked me to complete a task, I could quickly assess how much time I needed to get it done and if I could complete it before the given deadline. Whenever I was conflicted about needing more time to complete a task, I discussed it with my task lead or manager. This usually placed the prioritization of work on them to assess a more realistic timeline for delivery of solutions. Throughout my years of professional work experience, I've learned that communication is key when determining workload and prioritizing tasks to help ensure your success and performance credibility in the workplace.

When given multiple tasks or assignments, you may find it confusing to determine which assignment you should work to complete first. Let your task lead determine which assignment is of higher priority. Here are strategies to engage your task lead for prioritization of work when given additional assignments:

- "When do you need this assignment completed?"

    - This helps to determine if you have sufficient time to complete all of the assignments in your work queue by the scheduled deadlines.

- "Do you want me to work on this new assignment now, or after I complete assignment x?"

    - This reminds your task lead of the current work efforts on your plate. Task leads can be busy and responsible for several things, and they may forget all the assignments that you're supporting. This serves as a friendly reminder and places the prioritization on your task lead.

Nefisms

- Performance earns credibility.
- Performance creates an undisputed reputation.
- Constructive feedback can propel performance execution.
- Risks taken within your performance area can amass growth and development.
- Comprehension of unwritten rules can help you navigate performance obstacles.

2

Create Your Image

Creating your image in the workplace can be exciting. Why? Because you are the designer, crafting how people will perceive you physically. If you want to be taken seriously as a professional, you must take your image seriously. People in your office will tend to address you according to your presentation, so what you wear and how you wear it is important, and first impressions are critical.

Your image can make or break you in the workplace. Sad, but true! This is because the office is filled with human beings who are physical people living in a physical world, so image unfortunately matters. Keeping this in mind, you must brainstorm how you can best present yourself at work. Take some time to observe your colleagues and notice the attire of people currently in positions that you aspire to. Your workplace mentor, whom we'll talk about in Part Two: Strategic Relationships, will be a great resource. Ask him or her questions about how you should dress for work, what type of shoes are appropriate, etc.

Dress for Success

Your image in the workplace is heavily based on how you dress. If you want to win professionally, I strongly suggest that you dress for success. What does that mean? Here's a rule of thumb: dress today for the position you want tomorrow. Well, not literally tomorrow, but metaphorically. Dress today for the job you want three to five years from now. If you're bold, dress for the job you're strategizing to win ten years from now. If people in the workplace associate your attire with that of someone currently in the position you desire, then guess what? They'll naturally or even subconsciously begin to picture you as someone with the potential to assume that position one day. This is how powerful your image can be and why you should always dress for success.

My Approach to Dressing for Success

The night before each work day, I review my schedule for the next day. I look to see what types of meetings are on my calendar and with whom. Then I plan my attire based on the audience and the subject of the meeting. If I have a meeting with someone in a leadership position or a position of influence, I plan to wear a blazer. Likewise, if I have a critical meeting that discusses a serious matter, e.g. career development, program status meetings, or staff meetings, I will also wear a blazer. For such meetings, I intentionally focus on wearing clothing that projects a high level of professionalism. For a workday of general meetings, daily meetings, or no meetings at all, I tend to wear pleated slacks and a button-up shirt or a skirt and a nice blouse, as I'm a woman. Even further, as a woman, I routinely wear heels to work every day, or an occasional flat loafer, because heels silently exude a level of power and position.

Strategies to help you dress for success:

- Observe the attire of those in your workplace.
- Wear a button-up shirt and slacks.
- Wear a blazer when presenting or addressing a crowd.
- Wear shoes that nicely complement your attire.
- High-heeled shoes express a level of power—wear them if and when applicable.

- For women, wear a dress or skirt that falls to or below your knees.

Observing the attire of your colleagues is the first step towards dressing for success. You should aim to align your own style with the professional attire of your organization and company. If people in your organization wear a tie in the office, then you, too, should wear a tie to work. If they wear blazers in the office, then you should wear a blazer. Do you get it? If you're going to win in the workplace, then you have to align with the corporate image—this is playing it to win! How so? Because you have to look like you're a part of the team.

Wearing a button-up shirt and slacks is a step in the right direction when dressing for success. For maximum impact, ensure your button-up shirt is ironed and your slacks have pleats. Avoid wearing wrinkled shirts or pants because that would reduce the quality of your image and communicates your inability to present yourself as professional. People judge you based on what you wear.

When you're presented with an opportunity to address an audience, wear a blazer. A blazer communicates professionalism when standing before a crowd, helps to increase your confidence, and boosts your credibility.

Wearing shoes that nicely complement your attire will positively contribute to your total image. When observing you, the first thing people tend to look at is your shoes. Yes, shoes! Shoes communicate alot about a person's attention to detail, style, and comfort. Shoes arguably express an aspect of who you are without you opening your mouth. Therefore, be intentional about the shoes you wear.

For women, wearing high-heeled shoes expresses a level of power. When appropriate, wear a reasonable heel height that's suitable for your work environment. The rule of thumb is not to exceed a heel height of three inches. But with today's fashion trends, that can be challenging, so exercise good judgment or seek guidance from another woman in your workplace before wearing your desired high heels into the office.

Additionally, for women, when deciding what to wear to work, be aware of your dress and skirt length. The rule of thumb is for your hem to fall to or beneath your knees. Likewise, this could be challenging, given new fashion trends, but strive to find an appropriately conservative length for your work environment. When in doubt, reach out to another woman who you admire and ask for her guidance.

Never dress down on Friday! Remember, you're creating an image, and if you want your image to speak loudly, Fridays are the best days to do so. Why? Because people generally dress down and wear jeans or relaxed clothing on Fridays. However, since you're strategizing to win in the workplace, you will dress for success, even on a Friday. Dressing for success on a Friday draws attention to your image. It shows people that this is the image you present, even when others may not. As a result, it will influence people to take you more seriously.

Whenever you attend a social event organized by your company, always wear business casual. Why? Because business casual communicates that you are still representing the company in a good light, although the environment has changed. People in the workplace notice what you wear outside of business hours, so this is not the time to slack off. Use this opportunity to express through your image your ability to relax and still be a good representative of your company. This will help complement your performance at the office.

Your Image Should Complement Your Performance

Having a strong image to support your high performance will set you apart. This is one ingredient to help position you for success. Presenting yourself in a good light while solving problems in the workplace will eventually attract more opportunities to you. Such opportunities will allow you to grow and expand your skills; thus, you will evolve into a person of value. So you see, your image contributes to the type of opportunities you will attract to yourself.

How I Started Building My Evolving Image

After observing and studying my workplace and people within it for a year, I gained an understanding of the unwritten image an individual needed to possess to influence his or her success within the culture of the company. I first observed how individuals in leadership positions conducted themselves during meetings and their body language. I watched how they expressed themselves and how they engaged others. Then I paid close attention to how others in the meetings received and responded to the leader. This taught me, in real time, which tactics work and which ones don't work. I slowly began to incorporate these observations into my day-to-day interactions with people to help form my image and complement my execution as a high-performing employee. Next, I observed the consistent type of associations that successful individuals in leadership positions shaped. Then I gradually began to fashion similar types of associations at my level within the organization. This was the key ingredient, supplemented with my performance, that largely contributed to my image as a rising leader within the company.

Strategies to create an image that will complement your performance:

- Be aware of how you stand and how you sit during a meeting.
- Be cautious of your hand gestures.
- Pay attention to whom you associate with in the workplace.
- Acknowledge that perception is a reality until reality is known.
- Build executive presence.

Your posture expresses your level of confidence in yourself. Confidence is required to positively influence people in the workplace; how you stand while communicating your thoughts and ideas can largely influence how people receive your message. Therefore, stand tall whenever you're speaking and stand with your feet firmly planted. Your stance should express your confidence in yourself.

When attending a meeting that requires you to sit down, be mindful of your posture. Your sitting position also expresses your level of confidence. Therefore, sit with your back straight to express how confident you are—and if you're not confident, in this particular case, fake it 'til you make it. Sitting with good posture also helps you project your voice as you communicate your thoughts and ideas.

Whether you're sitting during a meeting or standing, be cautious of your hand gestures. Your hand gestures express your openness or resistance to other people's thoughts and ideas. Whether you agree or disagree with someone's thoughts, you should be open to hearing their perspective because strategizing to win in the workplace requires you to be open to the thoughts and ideas of others. Sometimes their perspective can help shape your approach to solving problems more efficiently. Further, when you use open hand gestures, you express yourself as an approachable person—someone with whom people feel comfortable talking, and they will form better relationships with someone they feel is approachable. When you use closed gestures, you express your disinterest in engaging in conversation, and this can create a space that makes people uncomfortable to exchange information with you. Therefore, because your use of hand gestures influences people's perception of your openness, use your hands effectively—this is playing it to win!

A workplace image is largely built through perception. Perception can literally create or destroy your brand and reputation because in many cases, perception is a reality until reality is known. For this reason, you must also be intentional about the associations you establish within the workplace because they can hinder or promote your growth and development within your organization or even across the company. Therefore, strive to form associations with individuals who share your level of performance and character. Play it to win by also associating with colleagues who can help you strategically reach your career goals and win in the workplace.

Aim to develop an image that can evolve into executive presence. Executive presence is a notion that communicates pinnacle qualities, such as the capability to lead and influence people. You do not need to be an executive to exude executive presence. Executive presence is a state of mind. People can feel it when someone possesses this presence, and that person can be at any level within the company. Executive presence is something that can be learned over time and built through exercise.

First Impressions

Whenever you're scheduled to meet someone for the first time, ensure you are dressed for success, especially if they are someone in a leadership position within your company. You will never get a second chance to make a first impression, so the first time is important.

Strategies to deliver effective first impressions:

- Offer a firm handshake.
- Make eye contact.
- Practice your 30-second elevator speech.
- Smile—it's contagious!

A firm handshake is expected when greeting someone in the workplace, especially for the first time. It expresses who you are and your level of confidence in who you are. Together with your name, a firm handshake introduces you before kick-starting a conversation. Professionals tend to make assumptions about you based on the firmness (or lack of firmness) in your handshake. So aim to give a firm handshake each time you greet someone. Remember, your handshake is a part of your introduction.

Always make eye contact. Eye contact is critical when interacting with people; it shows an individual that you are paying attention to them. This is pivotal because people want to believe they're being heard, especially when they are communicating their thoughts and ideas. Making eye contact with someone when they're talking shows them that they have your undivided attention. Likewise, you should make eye contact when you're talking. This helps express your level of confidence in yourself and in your thoughts and ideas.

The most popular way to make a first impression in the workplace is the 30-second elevator speech. This is a technique to introduce yourself to someone quickly. Given the 30-second time constraint, you should be able to communicate who you are and what you do in an effective way. Create a 30-second elevator speech and always be prepared to share it when you meet someone for the first time.

Smiling is contagious and will help attract people to you, especially when meeting them for the first time. People generally like those who smile because they project an approachable energy. When meeting someone for the first time, aim to exude a positive energy that encourages

others to want to learn more about you, what you do, and
your interests.

Nefisms

- An image is the beginning of an evolving perception.
- An image is a nonverbal communication that can precede your presence.
- An image can be shaped consciously or subconsciously.
- Intentionality can create a sustainable image.
- Advancement can be constrained by image.

3

Maximize Your Exposure

Exposure is key when starting and advancing in Corporate America. As a matter of fact, exposure is a necessity. Why? Because if no one knows who you are, then your performance and image are largely irrelevant. Collectively, performance, image, and exposure form the critical foundation to win in the workplace. Now, let's talk about why exposure is key.

Have you ever heard the saying, "It's not what you know but who you know?" Yeah, I've heard it too. In fact, people have been saying this for years—and it's partly true. But, before we discuss the whole truth, let's dissect this first. "It's not what you know but who you know" suggests that your associations can be more beneficial than your intelligence. Now, who you know is based on your level of exposure. Exposure is the act of communicating who you are and your value to an individual or group of people, generally those with some level of power or influence. Exposure provides an opportunity for others to learn about you. When others learn about your skills and talents, it creates a possibility for them to consider you for potential opportunities that may arise within their respective organizations or across the company.

As we mentioned before, to win in the workplace, you want to aim to be a high performer. However, one must be presented opportunities in order to perform, and that's partly why exposure is key. Exposure is the channel that connects your performance on the job and your image—how you present yourself to key people that can help you advance. Now, "who you know" has multiple levels. Yes, levels—generally, most things in life have levels. To win in the workplace, strive to diversify your exposure across as many levels of leadership and organizations as possible. Your goal is to become a household name, but in the workplace. People in your company should know that you are the person who does "this" and gets the job done while presenting yourself in a professional light. Your goals are to become a person of value and for others to know your value.

How I Started Growing My Visibility
within My Organization

As a new hire, I didn't know anyone at the company, but I knew I wanted to establish a network because that's what I was told to do in college. I always attended organizational meetings and arrived early to introduce myself to management or the facilitator and to offer to help solve any problem or issue I could support. I then followed up with them via email to schedule a one-on-one meeting to gain a better understanding of what they do and how I could help. In doing this, I grew my visibility across the management team of my organization.

Before organizational meetings, I also introduced myself to someone in the organization and made small talk. I asked them questions about their work and shared with them my contributions to the programs I was supporting. This approach sometimes transformed directly into opportunities for me or connected me to someone new, all as a result of the conversation. Given this tactic, I gradually started growing my visibility amongst the staff within my organization.

Additionally, I always attended social activities for my organization. I realized that my peers heavily attended these types of events, so I leveraged social activities as an opportunity to meet and develop relationships with my peer group. This inherently maximized my visibility within my organization. As my visibility increased, more opportunities to perform at a greater level where extended to me.

Strategies to grow your visibility within your organization:

- Attend a departmental lunch-and-learn.
- Volunteer to help support or organize critical activities for your organization.
- Attend quarterly departmental meetings held by management.
- Attend organizational meetings held by leadership.
- Participate in social activities within your organization.

Lunch-and-learns are generally technical exchange meetings that take place during lunch. Someone usually presents on a topic that's of interest to the attendees or shares content about a project, issue, or concern he or she is currently addressing. Lunch-and-learns are great settings to meet people within your organization. Since the meeting occurs during lunch, it's a relaxed environment in which people feel comfortable. Use it as an opportunity to introduce yourself to one or two people within your organization and express who you are, what you're currently working on, and your interests. This also allows you to learn about them as well as their technical expertise. This part is important because you need to learn whom to contact for technical guidance when you're faced with a particular type of problem. If you can match the right person to the technical need, then you increase the probability of solving a given problem, which will help increase your performance—that's how you play it to win.

Volunteering to help support or organize critical activities for your organization is a direct way to grow your visibility with leadership, management, and technical experts. Volunteering expresses your ability to extend yourself beyond your direct responsibilities to assist someone else. Organizational initiatives are usually derived from critical activities that require the support of staff at various levels to help achieve the identified goals. Since organizational initiatives are typically established by the leadership, they are highly visible, thus maximizing your exposure. Volunteer to support an activity in any capacity that you can, and be willing to learn new information and skills to support that activity.

Attending quarterly departmental meetings are a good opportunity to see everyone within your department and for them to know that you are also in their homeroom. Attending these meetings will inherently sustain your level of exposure. Over time, strive to meet and introduce yourself to everyone within your department. The goal is for them to know your area of expertise, so in the event that an opportunity arises that requires your skill set, they will think of you—that's the beauty of exposure.

Attending organizational meetings held by leadership is a great opportunity to learn the vision of your organization and how people within it are currently fulfilling that vision. Attending these meetings is important because you want to learn how you can directly contribute to the vision, which will help maximize your exposure. A strategic approach would be to introduce yourself to the individuals leading the effort and volunteer to support them in a capacity that supports your bandwidth. By building a good repertoire with these leaders, you will increase the probability of additional opportunities to expand your exposure across and maybe beyond your organization.

Participating in social activities within your organization is an exciting way to grow your exposure. Social activities create opportunities for you to learn about your coworkers beyond their roles and responsibilities. It allows you to learn about them as individuals, mature your established relationship with each of them, and vice versa. When you're able to connect with people on a personal level, they'll feel more comfortable with you and will be more likely to support you in various work capacities.

How I Started Growing My Visibility across My Company

As a new hire, I started growing my visibility across the company primarily through volunteerism. I first volunteered for the company-sponsored mentorship program with local high school students. This gave me an opportunity to help shape a young person's development, which I love, while providing me with a large networking opportunity. Through my participation in this company-sponsored program, I was able to establish relationships with various leaders at varying levels across the company. In parallel, I joined an Employee Resource Group (ERG) of like-minded individuals across the company who shared similar interests in addressing specific workplace concerns. This volunteer group connected me directly with people in management and leadership positions and created an opportunity to share my ideas and demonstrate my problem-solving skills amongst them. It also produced a platform for me to develop and exercise my leadership skills, which later led to an opportunity to join the company's cohort for rising leaders within the company.

These approaches to visibility led to game-changing opportunities that drastically increased my visibility at a rapid rate and launched my growing success.

Strategies to grow your visibility across your company:

- Join a functional community for your respective field.
- Join an Employee Resource Group (ERG).
- Attend company-sponsored events.
- Attend company all-hands meetings.
- Volunteer to support philanthropic activities.
- Volunteer to participate in mentorship programs.
- Volunteer to support recruitment activities.

Joining a functional community for your field within your company is a direct way to grow your professional exposure. A functional community is generally composed of people who share technical interests and skill sets at varying levels. This community will help you amplify your technical exposure and increase your awareness of opportunities that you can support across the company. To win in the workplace, get recognized for your performance within a particular domain. In other words, build a proven track record of delivering high performance in this specific area. Actively participating in a functional community creates a space for you to communicate your performance achievements, share best practices, and offer your skill sets to help solve problems company-wide—that's how you maximize your exposure while playing it to win.

Joining an Employee Resource Group (ERG) is a great way to maximize your exposure. An ERG is an internal club within your company that organizes events and meetings focused on addressing the concerns of its members. ERGs are a terrific avenue to gain and expand your exposure while establishing relationships with people who share common interests. These groups are inclusive, generally not constrained by profession, discipline, or area of expertise. Therefore, you can effortlessly gain access to an interdisciplinary network of people within your company, especially with those whom you may not typically encounter on a daily basis. This offers you maximum exposure and an opportunity to propagate your brand across multiple organizations without actually working or supporting the organizations directly. ERGs are an avenue to help you become a household name.

Company-sponsored events are generally professional social gatherings that require the attendance of business leadership. These events are great opportunities to network with individuals at high levels on the organizational chart. Attending company-sponsored events provides you the opportunity to meet various people within your organization and throughout your company, with a specific focus on leadership. Aim to introduce yourself to as many people in business leadership positions as possible. Your goal is to gain their business cards with the intention of scheduling information sessions—that's an approach to strategically expand your exposure to business leadership.

Attending company-sponsored events is also a fun and festive way to grow your exposure. Holiday parties are popular company-sponsored events; they are a great way to meet people across the company while enjoying yourself. Socializing in this way also provides you the opportunity to nurture existing relationships that you can leverage strategically in the future to help you advance.

All-hands meetings are critical to gain insight into the direction of your company. During an all-hands meeting, the business' focal areas are discussed in detail. All employees are invited to these meetings, and it's a great opportunity to introduce yourself to someone you've been waiting for an opportunity to meet—in particular, a business leader. Aim to sit as close to the front as possible to increase the probability of meeting that individual. When you meet them, give your 30-second elevator speech and then ask to schedule a follow-up meeting— this is an approach to establishing an information session, which we'll discuss later in greater detail.

Additionally, volunteering to support philanthropic activities such as toy drives, school drives, coat drives, etc. is a fulfilling way to engage with people across your company while supporting good causes. In the workplace, participating in volunteer work helps demonstrate your authentic character and willingness to help others, which is one key to winning in the workplace. Through volunteer work, you gain access to people across varying disciplines and organizations, which maximizes your exposure to new people and new opportunities.

Volunteering to participate in your company's mentorship program is a strategic way to pay it forward while shining light on your ability to influence and shape the development of others. Gaining exposure to and experience in the professional development of others will help shape your leadership qualities. It also prepares you to lead technical and functional teams in your future. This is key as you grow within your career. Acting as a mentor helps increase your exposure, as these programs are generally not domain- or discipline-focused but inclusive of everyone across the company.

Volunteering to support recruitment activities is a great way to learn about your company's hiring strategy and initiatives while allowing human resources to learn more about your skills and experience. To win in the workplace, you must establish relationships and gain exposure amongst individuals within the human resources department. Why? Because the human resources department is essentially the heartbeat of the company. It is their job to become aware of the skill sets needed to address the needs of each organization within the company, then identify the talent that can meet that need. Human resources staff are also responsible for succession planning. Succession planning is the process of identifying a talent pool with the potential to lead critical areas of the company and then developing those individuals' potential into tangible skills through direct or indirect guided experiences. By establishing relationships with people in human resources and volunteering to support recruitment activities, you can share with them your current skills and experience and inquire about available opportunities that can help grow your skill sets and further your level of exposure. This also increases the probability of them considering you for new opportunities when they arise, especially for opportunities related to succession planning.

Your Brand Promotion

Exposure also helps promote your brand. You have a brand in the workplace, whether it's intentional or unintentional. When starting in your company, intentionally create your brand. You should aim to control the perception and associations that are made or even inferred when your name arises in conversation. How do you do this? By delivering a high level of performance on all tasks and consistently presenting a professional image. It takes time to build a brand in the workplace, and conversely, someone's brand in the workplace can be destroyed at any moment—so consistency and situational awareness are key!

My Approach to Creating My Brand in the Workplace

In the workplace, I want my brand to represent the characteristics and qualities of the best version of myself. I strive to develop the brand of an individual who is knowledgeable, resourceful, driven, always professionally dressed, an excellent communicator, willing to help others, a pleasure to work with, and a team player. Each day, I aim to promote these attributes by exhibiting them in the workplace through my interactions with others.

Remember, I said, "It's not what you know but who you know" is only partly true? The truth is, "It's not who you know, but who knows you." These sayings are similar but subtly different, and together, they equal the whole truth of exposure. You see, almost everyone knows Oprah, but out of those people, who does Oprah actually know? If the person with power or influence knows who you are, it most likely increases your chances of being presented with opportunities to help you advance in the workplace. So your next question should be, "Well, how do I get Oprah to know me?" The answer is through an information session, which we'll discuss next.

Information Sessions

A highly effective approach to gain exposure is through information sessions. From the perspective of exposure, the information session serves as an avenue to gain insight into the person you're meeting with during a one-on-one encounter, and that individual can do the same.

My Approach to Information Sessions

Whenever I'm looking to gain a new mentor or strategically position myself on the radar of someone in a position of power or influence, I schedule an information session. From my personal experience, I've gained both mentors and sponsors as a result of information sessions. Additionally, I've gained a better understanding of career navigation from the individuals with whom I've conducted information sessions. Further, I gained insight into new and developing initiatives across the company, which created opportunities for me later.

Strategies to schedule an information session:

- Email a person of interest; introduce yourself and request an information session of 30 minutes to an hour.

  - This approach works best for someone you've previously met at an open forum and with whom you have been looking to follow up.

- Send a meeting notification for an information session of 30 minutes to an hour.

  - This approach works for someone you already know or may have had a number of encounters with, from whom you are seeking to gain more insight.

How to prepare for an information session:

- Determine what you want to accomplish in this meeting.

  - Do you want him or her to become your mentor or sponsor?

  - Do you need their guidance to help you navigate an obstacle you're currently facing?

  - Do you need them to recommend you for a new opportunity?

- Do you need to gain insight into an area of the organization with which you're currently unfamiliar?

- Do you want to offer your services to help them solve any problems or concerns they're currently facing?

- Never show up misinformed.

  - Read the person's biography.

  - Learn their position within the organizational chart.

  - Always prepare questions to ask.

  - Identify ways you can help them do their job more effectively.

Nefisms

- Exposure attracts new opportunities.
- Exposure creates a platform for service.
- Exposure demands a greater version of yourself.
- Lack of preparation can minimize exposure.
- Perception can influence your level of exposure.

Part Two

Strategic Relationships

Consider it a marathon, not a sprint. Those who endure to the end shall win, so you need the right people to help you get there.

4

Establish a Relationship with Management

Your management chain is critical to your development within the company. These individuals can either promote or stunt your career growth—that's how much positional power they have. They are the individuals who largely influence your upward mobility within their organization, so recognizing how influential these people are to your career is important if you are to take the necessary steps to establish meaningful relationships that can support your advancement.

Establish a Relationship with Your Direct Manager

Your manager is a vital player in your development. He or she should always be a top priority. This is largely because they assess and evaluate your annual performance which influences your ability to be promoted to the next level, gain salary increases, and receive incentives such as performance-based awards. Do you see why this person is vital? Your manager also approves your training and vacation requests, which is absolutely necessary when you need time away from the office. He or she is also involved to some degree in your pursuit and attainment of new opportunities, which will help you become a game-changer.

How I Established a Relationship with My Manager

When I was assigned a new manager, I scheduled a one-on-one to get to know him and to share information about myself. We discussed professional topics such as his academic background, career experiences at the company, and the culture of the company itself. I too shared my academic background and professional experience to date. We later discussed my career interests and the type of opportunities that were of interest to me. This first meeting set the tone for a growing professional relationship.

To nurture my relationship with my manager, I always keep him abreast of the latest updates concerning the work I performed. Whenever something positively or negatively impacted my work, I communicated it to him early which increased the effectiveness of managing me as a direct report. Additionally, I expressed gratitude when my manager helped resolve issues on my behalf and sought out new opportunities for me. Further, I reached out to him monthly, simply to check in with him. This created an opportunity to provide him with a status update, to see how he's doing, and to hear about his work.

Strategies to establish a successful relationship with your direct manager:

- Cultivate a trusted relationship.
- Develop interest in his or her personal life.
- Demonstrate your ability to be accountable and reliable.
- Assist your manager with low-bearing department efforts.
- Be inquisitive about your manager's professional roles and responsibilities.
- Praise him or her when applicable.

Acknowledging that your manager is vital in your development necessitates that you cultivate a professional level of trust with him or her. Your manager should be able to trust and rely on you, and your working relationship with him or her should reflect this. Establishing such a relationship takes time, but it will yield success if you nurture it intentionally.

Take time to learn about your manager's personal life. If you're going to cultivate a trusting relationship with them, then you need to create a comfortable space for professional reasons. Never pry into the details of your manager's life, but do express earnest interest in the things they share with you. Be authentic in your interactions with your manager, because most people can smell a "brownnoser," and that's frowned upon.

Demonstrate that you are accountable and reliable by carrying out your commitments. When you commit to doing something, you must fulfill it. Aim to exhibit your levels of accountability and reliability to your manager whenever possible. You want him or her to know that you mean what you say and say what you mean. You can also demonstrate accountability and reliability by executing tasks given to you and completing those tasks on time.

Assisting your manager with low-bearing department efforts is also a good way to strengthen your relationship. By offloading mundane tasks, you relieve them of the burden and provide them with more time to take care of more important efforts. Granted, the mundane tasks may have some level of significance, but they are likely less demanding than their other responsibilities. When you have the bandwidth to help your manager, first help with these tasks. In the process, you may gain exposure from your organizational leadership since it's a departmental effort—this is playing it to win, killing two birds with one stone.

Be inquisitive about your manager's professional roles and responsibilities. Show that you're interested in their work. Although your manager is hierarchically responsible for you, they are still an employee just like you and have professional goals and aspirations. Therefore, support your manager in their goals whenever you have the bandwidth to assist, and they will likely return the favor. Note, the success of your professional relationship should be bi-directional when it comes to support; you shouldn't be the only one reaping the benefits of this working relationship.

Furthermore, praising your manager is a great way to mature your relationship with him or her. Recognizing your manager amongst their peers and especially their leadership will help to strategically position you for success. Most people in the workplace want to be recognized for their contribution and efforts, so praising your manager should be a top priority for you. Of course, the praise should be authentic and delivered when applicable, so use your discernment and don't be a brownnoser.

Establish a Relationship with Your Manager's Direct Manager

In addition to establishing a trustful relationship with your manager, you should also strive to establish a professional relationship with your manager's direct manager. Yes, the second relationship with management is necessary because your manager usually has to get an endorsement from his manager before he can approve your requests. This is generally how hierarchical organizations operate. Therefore, if you work within a pyramid-structured organization, understanding how such a tiered structure functions necessitates establishing a relationship with your manager's direct manager. It's simply the nature of the corporate beast.

Your relationship with your manager's direct manager does not need to be as professionally intimate as the relationship with your manager. However, you should strive to be intentional in developing an authentic working relationship with him or her. Stop by your manager's direct manager's office at least twice a month, simply to say hello and have a brief chat. However, you rarely want to share information or concerns with your manager's direct manager without first discussing it with your direct manager. This is a no-no; you always want to respect your manager by keeping him or her updated with the latest content concerning you, as opposed to your manager receiving information from someone else, especially someone ranked higher in the hierarchy. How disrespectful would that be? Basically, it's your unwritten responsibility to keep your manager abreast of information before he or she is faced with it directly. This ideology will ultimately help to better serve you and your career endeavors within the organization and across the company.

Whenever you're meeting with your manager's direct manager and he or she shares information with you that may concern you either positively or negatively, immediately update your manager with this information after the conversation—this is how your manager will gain more respect for you and value you more highly. Remember, your manager must stay abreast of information pertaining to you in order to positively influence your career growth.

How I Established a Relationship with My Manager's Boss

After establishing a developing relationship with my manager, I started to initiate a relationship with my manager's boss. This relationship is key because my manager must get guidance or endorsement from his boss in order to approve many of my requests. So I thought establishing a relationship with him would help streamline any future requests I might have regarding career development. I started by stopping by his office, simply to say hi or asking him how his weekend was. Many times, he invited me into his office for a short conversation, during which I started updating him on my current tasks. Over time, I established a working relationship with him almost to the same degree of my direct manager. As a result of this growing relationship, I noticed that many of my career development requests were routinely approved, all while I was gaining further insight into available opportunities within the organization as a result of our discussions.

Strategies to establish a successful relationship with the manager of your direct manager:

- Develop interest in their personal life.
- Help them achieve their organizational goals.
- Acknowledge your direct manager when talking with his or her manager about opportunities.

Developing interest in their personal life is a great way to begin establishing a relationship. You can do this by inquiring about their weekend and then pulling the thread on things shared within the conversation to learn more about them. Then, the next time you see them, ask about something they mentioned in your previous conversation. After that, pull the thread on things shared in this conversation to learn even more. As a result, you're creating a mental database of interests and information about this individual's personal life, which will allow you to be authentically interested in the person.

Learn the organizational goals of the manager of your direct manager so you can support their efforts to achieve them. This is a great approach to establishing a relationship with someone within your management team who isn't your direct manager. By directly contributing to his or her organizational goals, you become valuable because you are helping them fulfill their responsibilities while developing and maturing a professional relationship. Whenever you're able to help someone in the workplace accomplish their goals, you become an asset—this is playing it to win.

Acknowledge your direct manager when talking with his or her manager about opportunities. This demonstrates your professional respect for your manager and expresses your ability to exude professional loyalty to leadership. This is a great character quality to possess, especially when developing a relationship with management. It also shows that you desire that your manager know of activity concerning you, which is frankly, his or her job. It further shows that you understand the organizational construct and culture of the company. As a result, this manager discerns that they can trust you with opportunities and responsibilities outside of their direct organization.

Establish a Relationship with the Leadership of Your Organization

The manager of your manager's direct manager may be in a leadership position over your respective organization. He or she is likely the decision-maker for the operation and functionality of your organization, so you have to establish some level of relationship. Why? Because he or she most likely grants the distribution of salary increases, promotions, and employee incentives within the organization, while influencing who should be sponsored for new opportunities. Stopping by this person's office at least once a month simply to say hello will help him or her put a face to your name for the times when your manager and manager's direct manager praise you or make a request for you during internal organizational meetings.

Do not feel pressured to establish a strong relationship with this person but form a relationship to some degree. Why? Because you have to set yourself apart from your peers within the organization. By ensuring that they know who you are and are familiar with your personality and professionalism, they will be more willingly to endorse and recommend you when opportunities and requests arise.

How I Established a Relationship with My Leadership Team

After establishing a solid and developing relationship with my direct manager, then a growing relationship with his boss, I thought it would be worthwhile to establish light relationships with the individuals on my leadership team. I knew this team would hear about my work contributions from status meetings with their direct staff, but I wanted to provide them with the opportunity to put a face with my name. So every two to three weeks, I simply walked by their offices just to say hi and ask, "How are you doing?" Usually, if time permitted, they invited me in for a brief conversation and asked me about my work and my overall experience at the company. As a result, when opportunities became available, they recommended and endorsed me through my chain of management. I quickly realized that having a relationship with my entire chain of management positioned me for career growth.

Strategies to establish a successful relationship with the leadership of your organization:

- Develop interest in his or her personal life.
- Learn their organizational goals so you can support their efforts.
- Acknowledge your direct manager when talking with his or her leadership about opportunities.

As with your direct manager and your manager's direct manager, you must develop a level of interest in this higher-level manager's personal life. Establishing this particular relationship is key because he or she will have great influence upon your upward mobility within the organization and perhaps the company overall.

It's very critical that you learn the organizational goals of your leadership so you can support their efforts. These specific goals impact you, your direct manager, and his or her manager. Therefore, finding ways to help support these goals will strategically position you for success. Explore ways in which you can directly impact their goals and identify how you can gain the bandwidth to do so. These activities will be significant to your growth as you gain direct exposure and as the leadership of your organization becomes directly familiar with your skills and accountability.

Acknowledge your direct manager when talking with his leadership about opportunities, just as when you're talking with his or her manager. Again, you must demonstrate your professional level of respect for your manager while indirectly reminding leadership who your direct manager is. This is key because when an opportunity arises, you want your organizational leadership to know how to get access to you. Many times, opportunities for your development are discussed with your direct manager before they're even presented to you—this tends to be the case in hierarchal organizations.

So acknowledging your direct manager becomes key when talking with organizational leadership.

Nefisms

- Professional relationships influence upward mobility.
- Professional relationships established authentically can produce positive fruit.
- Professional relationship growth necessitates effort.
- Trustworthiness cultivates professional relationships.
- Information exchange can help sustain professional relationships.

5

Know Your Organizational Chart

The organizational chart, also known as the "org chart", is a hierarchical view of the organization and company. It displays a professional headshot or list of people in leadership positions—the who's who within your company. It also shows horizontal and vertical positions of leadership. The org chart is a visible and valuable representation of the company structure and a resource with which you should familiarize yourself.

Familiarize Yourself with the CEO, President, and Executive Board

As an employee of the company, you should be able to identify the Chief Executive Officer (CEO). The CEO is the appointed leader of the company and with the help of his or her counsel, is responsible for establishing the direction of the company, which inherently impacts you. So if you fail to memorize anyone else on the org chart, please at least know the face and name of the CEO. For traditional corporations, there generally exists a President who presides over each sector of the company. The President carries out the direction of the CEO for their respective sector—yet another name and face you should memorize. Most Presidents have an Executive Board, that consists of Vice Presidents (VPs). The VPs lead the business units of the sector. You should be able to identify each VP of the sector you work within. I know, more names and faces to memorize, but it's ultimately for your success. Be able to match executive names with faces, so you're well positioned in the event that you're in their presence or whenever their name comes up in workplace conversation. Most importantly, be able to recognize your direct VP, the shepherd of the sheep. This is key because you need to know who is the leader that largely influences the direction of your business area. If an opportunity arises, introduce yourself to him or her and schedule an information session. You see, I told you this was for your success. The goal is to be in position for when an opportunity presents itself, to chat about the direction of the business area and identify ways in which you can support this direction—this is playing it to win!

My Approach to Learning and Meeting People on My Org Chart

During one day at work, I was having a candid conversation with one of my peers in the office, and she mentioned a VP's name. I had no idea who that person was or the fact that he was a VP. Next, she mentioned another VP's name, and again I was lost. She then asked me, "Nef, do you know who your VP is?" To my dismay, I said no. She immediately opened her web browser, navigated to our company's intranet, and opened our executive management organizational chart. She looked me straight in the eyes and boldly said, "You need to know your org chart."

Once I learned how to find the org charts online, I started memorizing names and positions, as well as who reported to whom. As I was learning my org chart, I would attend various work functions and see some of the faces from the charts. This created a perfect opportunity for me to join small networking conversations that they were a part of, then subsequently introduce myself—in a seamless yet cordial fashion. This approach yielded me a number of information sessions with executive management, which collectively brought my org chart navigation to life and helped me gain a better understanding of the company and its direction from the highest levels.

Your Department Organizational Chart

Similar to your company's overarching org chart, you should learn your department org chart. This one should be much easier to learn since you likely see these folks more frequently. Be able to identify the leadership and recognize the managers within your department. Because your department is home base, at least be able to pronounce these people's names correctly. Knowing where you sit within the department and who your verticals are will serve you well, especially when sharing and exchanging information with people in the workplace. Basically, you need to know who reports to whom and who has power and influence in making a decision that ultimately impacts you. Therefore, know your org charts!

Nefisms

- Knowledge prepares you for the moment to come.
- Knowledge better positions you for execution.
- Knowledge enlightens your perspective.
- Information enhances knowledge.
- Resources can be leveraged to supplement knowledge.

6

Identify and Build
Your Team

As soon as you start in the workplace, you want to build your team. You need a team of people who can contribute to your growth and advancement. Have you ever heard the saying, "It takes a village to raise a child" or "No one becomes successful on his or her own"? Well, it's true! One person cannot solely raise a child into a functioning adult, and likewise, you cannot reach the pinnacle of success on your own merit alone. Therefore, take time to identify your team.

Who Is a Sponsor?

A sponsor is someone in a position of power and influence who can endorse you for opportunities. This person is your champion when opportunities arise. Take a moment to visualize your champion as a cheerleader. He or she can nominate and root for you at high levels within the organization and across the company. A sponsor is typically someone who admires your skills and character and is able to recognize your potential to advance up the corporate ladder, which is a fantastic thing. Further, most sponsors see characteristics of themselves in the people whom they sponsor, which inclines them to inspire and encourage you towards greater success.

Who Is a Mentor?

A mentor is typically someone in a management position who can give you strategic guidance and teach you the corporate culture of the company. Take a moment to visualize your mentor as a coach. He or she wants to invest in your development and help you avoid obstacles. This person also wants to help you navigate challenges that you may face as you learn and adjust to the corporate politics of the company, which is absolutely critical to your success. Additionally, this person can provide you organizational insight and help you strategize to win.

Vertical and Horizontal People from the Organizational Chart

Establishing a team that will lead you towards success requires strategy. At a minimum, your team needs to include both vertical and horizontal people. Vertical and horizontal—what does that mean? It means that you need to identify people who are in roles above and below your position in the workplace hierarchy, as well as people who are in lateral positions to you. I have already discussed why you should establish relationships with managers in a position of power or influence above your level, but you need to also establish relationships with people who have less positional power than you because these people actually influence your success. Why? They most likely report to you or collaborate with you on tasks; therefore, in many cases, you're not successful unless they are successful. This is also true for establishing relationships with people who share power with you in lateral positions. Moreover, those who have more positional power than you will sometimes ask your peers or those below you in the org chart to describe or assess your character and performance. Not everyone who sits at the top believes the hype about you, so be prepared for them to randomly inquire through those who sit below and across from you in the hierarchy about you as a contributor and as an individual. This is yet another reason why building a team to support your success is important.

Identifying Your Vertical Advocate

Now that you understand the construct of vertical and horizontal people, it's time to identify your team. Every team has a starting line-up, so determine yours. First, strategically identify your verticals. Let's begin by finding your sponsors. You want a man in a leadership position who is respected by his peers based on his talent and character. This is important because if people respect him based on his character, they will also respect the decisions and recommendations that he makes, such as sponsoring you for opportunities that can develop your skills and experience while giving you illuminating exposure. Then you want to identify a woman in a leadership position with the same level of respect. Be strategic! Aim to identify a woman who's socially embraced by her peers. Having both male and female sponsorship in leadership positions will gain you access to superb opportunities and will advance your career. These folks will be your "known" sponsors.

Next, identify a vertical person in a management role who sits two to three positions above you in the hierarchy. This person will be your mentor.

Then identify a vertical person who sits below you in the hierarchy. This should be someone in whom you see a lot of potential and someone who shares your similar drive and career ambition. It's important to mentor someone as you grow and advance upward. As you're seeking people above you to bless you with opportunities, you must also be willing to simultaneously create opportunities for others. This will not only help you pay it forward, but it will also illustrate your ability to contribute to the growth of others, which is key if you want to climb the corporate ladder. Further, when working, you always want to identify someone who can be your successor. You never want to transition from a position without recommending a good replacement, and the person you're mentoring can sometimes be a good successor, depending upon their skills and background.

How I Identified My Vertical Advocates

Establishing my vertical advocates was quite organic. They were all naturally attracted to me as a result of my high performance and volunteerism in company-sponsored activities, which is a general way to initially meet and later gain sponsors and mentors. After a number of small chats during networking functions over the course of a year, I asked my potential advocates if I could schedule quarterly meetings with them for career guidance and navigation. They responded positively, and this is how I secured my vertical advocates.

Identifying Your Horizontal Advocate

So where are we now with our starting lineup? We have identified two people in leadership positions who are our sponsors, one person in a management position who is our mentor, and one person who sits below us in the hierarchy who is our mentee. Now we need one more person to fill the remaining position to establish a starting five lineup at minimum. This position should be filled by someone in a lateral position. Identify one male or female, but be strategic. Be very strategic here! People who sit in lateral positions usually want the same thing that you want—to get promoted to the next level. And guess what? If you both are laterals in the same department, sometimes only one of you can gain the promotion. So that's why you must be very strategic. However, you still need laterals for collaboration, because collaboration is a key component to winning in the workplace.

At this point, you're probably thinking, well, why do I need my laterals to help me succeed when they're essentially my competition? You're right; your performance is generally evaluated against and compared to those in similar positions. But here's the trick with laterals. Come closer! You need a strategic partner who can advocate for you and endorse an idea or approach that will help create an opportunity for you. Granted, the opportunity may be shared between the two of you, which will later require that you divide and conquer. However, without this individual's endorsement, your initiative may be at risk of being realized. How so? Because when two or more are in agreement, it increases the viability of the proposition.

How I Identified My Horizontal Advocates

Identifying my horizontal advocates was much more challenging than establishing my vertical advocates. Perhaps my cautiousness to trust folks in the workplace contributed to the level of difficulty. Many would consider this a simple choice, but I personally disagree. It took me time to relax my reservations to the level at which I could gain a trusted workplace peer. Through time, observation, and discernment, I naturally gravitated towards an individual with whom I built a working relationship as a horizontal advocate and eventually a workplace friend.

Congratulations! You now have a team assembled to help you win in the workplace.

Schedule a Regimen for Meeting with Your Team

Now that you have assembled your team, you need to develop a cadence for meeting with each individual. Remember, your team is going to help you win the chess game of Corporate America, so you have to be intentional about the frequency of your discussions.

My Approach for Meeting with My Advocates

I meet with my sponsors once a quarter for an hour. I meet with my mentors bi-monthly for an hour. However, whenever I need help resolving an issue, I reach out to one of my mentors directly. In regard to my horizontal advocates, I usually chat with them daily, at minimum once a week. This regimen has worked rather well for me. During my meetings with my vertical advocates, I share what's going on with me, what challenges I was able to overcome, and what my current interests are. I also ask for advice concerning any topics or problems I may have. My meetings with my horizontal advocates are drastically different. We simply chat about various topics, work-related and non-work-related. We also exchange thoughts and ideas on issues and situations related to programs we support. My meetings with horizontal advocates provide opportunities to have a conversation with someone who understands where I'm coming from and can sympathize with me.

Proposed meeting cadence for your team:

- Sponsor
  - Once a quarter – four times a year
- Mentor
  - Bimonthly – six times a year
- Mentee
  - Bimonthly – six times a year
- Lateral
  - Weekly or more often as necessary

Nefisms

- Professional partnerships encourage growth and development.
- Professional partnerships offer new perspectives.
- Professional partnerships can help reveal blind spots in an execution.
- Advocacy can be more impactful through professional partnerships.
- Elevation can be established through professional partnerships.

7

Learn the Cliques in the Workplace

OMG! Just when you thought cliques were over in high school, and maybe you even thought they were obsolete in college, here they are again, but now in the workplace. Listen, I don't like cliques any more than you do, but if you're going to win in the workplace, you must play the game, and unfortunately, that requires learning about the cliques in the workplace and maybe even joining one or two.

Observation Is Key

When you first arrive in the workplace, take some time to observe. Observation is your first step before you take any action or open your mouth. It's a crucial key if you want to win in the workplace.

The most important observations should start in your department. You need to get the "tea" on how opportunities are created and allocated, where the money comes from and how it's distributed, and who are best at their jobs. Finally, you need to know who are the decision-makers, the advocates, and those who influence or rather have the eyes and ears of the decision-makers. Now that's alot to learn, and you won't gain this type of intellectual capital overnight, but with time you will learn everything you need to know generally through observation or from people "spilling tea" around the office.

Observation through Team Differentiation

Next to observations, the best way to learn the cliques in the workplace is by working with different teams. When you work with different teams, you are exposed to different groups of people, and you have an opportunity to learn more about the individuals you're working with. You will learn more about each individual's interests, perspectives, character, and their levels of relationship with others within the department—that last one is key, because that helps unlock the discovery of cliques within the workplace. Learning who is "friends" with whom is the knowledge needed to mature your strategy to win within the workplace. Now sometimes you don't have to be "friends" with the entire clique. Rather, you just need to be "friends" with at least one person within the clique who will speak well about you amongst the others. Remember, a strategy is key here! You don't want to exhaust yourself with the burden of befriending and establishing relationships with everyone you meet. You still need energy to perform at a level that exceeds expectations. Therefore, be strategic in who you befriend and make it meaningful and authentic.

My Approach to Observation through Team Differentiation

When I join a new team, I initially spend time observing the team dynamics. When I joined my current program, I spent the first month lightly observing each person and paying close attention to collaborations and small chats. This helped me to develop an understanding of the various levels of relationships amongst individuals on the team. With tact, I leveraged my ongoing observations to position myself to support individuals who would speak well and with great impact on my behalf.

Observation through Social Interaction

Workplace social gatherings are a great way to learn about the cliques in the workplace. When most people gather in a social environment, they tend to "let their hair down," at least to some degree. At the social gathering, people within a clique will typically gather together just to have idle chitchat. People also tend to gather around others with whom they feel comfortable, and members of a clique definitely feel comfortable in each other's company, so watch for them! I recommend finding a place in the room that gives you a good vantage point of the crowd, then observe. While you're people-watching, take mental notes of everything! And as more social events arise, continue to attend them to help validate the observations you've made over the course of time.

My Approach to Observation through Social Interaction

I've discovered that the best way to identify cliques in the workplace is at social events. I strive to attend as many social activities as possible, not only for the networking aspect and to learn more about folks outside of the office, but to also observe the level of personal relationships individuals have established. I previously attended a Friendsgiving event organized by one of my peers. Several folks from the office were there, and to my surprise, many of them were super close with each other. That day I discovered cliques and relationships I hadn't been exposed to in the workplace. When I returned to the office, I had a better understanding of who was connected to whom and at what diverse levels.

Expanding Your Observation

After you've acquired a good understanding of the cliques within your department, it's time to expand your observation across the company. It doesn't matter if your company is big or small, be strategic in your expansion. Target an area, organization, or team that could contribute to the continual development of your skills and experience.

One of the best ways to expand your observation is by supporting volunteer events across various organizations. Why? Because people generally don't refuse free help, so it's the best way to get your foot into the door.

My Approach to Expanding My Observation

I've learned that a good way to expand my observation across the company is through volunteerism. Almost no one in the workplace turns down free help or a lending hand. I discovered a tiger team within the company that was leading an initiative that was of interest to me, and I volunteered to help the team accomplish their goals. This team was composed of high-performing employees at various levels and across several organizations. Through my support for the team, I gained a better understanding of the company and established relationships across many organizations. This insight boosted my ability to better navigate the culture of the company.

Nefisms

- Observation enhances the strategy to tackle obstacles.
- Observation triggers adaptability.
- Observation exposes intentionality.
- Execution can be influenced by observation.
- Advancement can be impacted by peer observation.

8

Find a "Best Friend" at Work

As you become more knowledgeable of the workplace, you want to find someone who shares your drive and aspirations for success. Somewhat similar to a tag-team partner. This person should be able to sharpen you like iron and be a great source for exchanging valuable information. In fact, the acquisition of valuable information is needed to win in the workplace. So having someone you can trust to some extent will help grow your repository information in the workplace.

Benefits of a "Best Friend" at Work

A peer mentor or "best friend" at work will help you to better navigate the workday. Having a best friend at work helps spark excitement in your day. Knowing that this person is going to bring you a source of relief when work is stressful or tiresome will give you encouragement. This person can also serve as a sounding board when you're strategizing ways to win in the workplace, which gives you a different perspective. It's always great to have someone you can talk to who is similar in age, shares your level of maturity, character, and lifestyle, or who understands your challenges—relatability is key here! These qualities are what will draw you together and perhaps qualify the relationship to exchange information at a level of your comfort.

How I Selected My Best Friend at Work

When I joined the company, I didn't set out to find a best friend at work. However, through employee engagement activities, it was suggested that employees who have a best friend at work have a more enjoyable time. I didn't pay much attention to this, but over time I naturally developed a good relationship with a few people in the workplace, whom I now consider best friends at work. I met each individual through company-sponsored volunteer activities. I believe our shared passion for Science, Technology, Engineering, and Mathematics (STEM) outreach is where we connected and we later built relationships through lunches and random Skype messages throughout the day.

I don't believe one sets out to find a best friend at work. Instead I think it's a relationship that evolves organically and makes coming into the office more exciting.

Selecting a "Best Friend" at Work

You must choose your "best friend" wisely. However, never trust anyone wholeheartedly because the workplace is a game, and there are no real friends in a competition. Always be mindful that you come to work to get the job done and you have true friends at home. On the surface, this sounds doable, but as you begin to establish relationships with people in the workplace, you will find that you share similarities, views, and perspectives with a number of people. Your shared ability to relate to each other will make it rather difficult not to express some level of transparency. This is simply because you're a human being, so connecting with other people to some extent is inevitable. However, you must be cautious and always exercise a level of discernment.

Exercise caution when selecting and sharing personal or professional information with your "best friend." You never want to share information that you would not mind reading on the cover of the *Washington Post* in the morning. Using this analogy as a rule of thumb will help guide you in your dialogue exchange. Also, it may be helpful to establish boundaries for sharing information. Know what you are willing to talk about and what is off limits. Never share any information that could potentially make you personally or professionally vulnerable. Use your instincts, discernment, and intuition to guide you within this relationship.

Nefisms

- Professional friendships can create an enjoyable work experience.
- Professional friendships encourage professional accountability.
- Professional friendships can develop over time.
- Organic professional friendships are shaped without motive.
- Strengths and talents can be identified through professional friendships.

Part Three

Strategic Planning

Success is planned. Set goals that will lead you towards your aspirations.

9

Identify a Career Track

A career track outlines a trail towards the position you aspire to. A company typically offers various career tracks to help guide you in determining your career aspirations, and this is actually a good thing. Career tracks are templates that abstractly describe the recommended skills and experiences an individual should possess in order to advance towards the desired position. Most are generic, simple templates. However, identifying a career track provides you with a target and a path to begin developing the essential skills needed to function in your ultimate desired role. When you identify a career track, you gain the benefit of positioning yourself for intentional experiences that will shape the trajectory of your career. This is beneficial because intentionality is required for sustainable success. Additionally, a career track will help you establish a level of purpose for your career. When you establish a level of purpose, you attract the people, resources, and opportunities that will help you grow beyond measure.

Matching Your Interests to Available Career Tracks

Within your first month of starting in the workplace, obtain the company's available career tracks. The career tracks are usually accessible through the company's intranet, an internal employee-only website, but your manager can also share with you where to find it. Spend time on your own reviewing the career tracks and pondering what seems to be of interest to you. Meet with your manager and mentors to discuss the career tracks and your career interests. Granted, you most likely won't know which exact career track you want to pursue upon starting in Corporate America, but based upon your education and interests, you can eliminate a number of unrelated tracks. Also, your manager and mentors will be able to provide you with insight into the career tracks based on their experience and years of service within the company.

How I Leveraged My Interests to Explore Career Tracks

After completing five summer internships, as well as undergraduate research and graduate research through my master's thesis, I possessed a clear understanding of my interests when I started my career as a full-time, professional employee. I leveraged my previous workplace exposure to rule out tracks that were of no interest to me. Early on, my interests in the workplace were to develop into a technical leader. Not just any technical leader, but to become a knowledgeable technical leader with respected subject matter expertise and impactful technical contributions. I also wanted to be a proficient communicator with high emotional intelligence and a strong ability to lead and empower people. With such interests, I explored the company's available career tracks that best aligned with the proposed evolution of my professional development.

Who can help you match your skills and talents to available career tracks?

- Your management team
- Mentors
- Sponsors

Your management team is responsible for helping you identify your career track, but you must be proactive in initiating the discussion and seeking their assistance. Your direct manager is available to you to help you shape your career, but you need to be able to communicate your interests and passions so he or she can advise you accordingly. Since the individuals within your management team are at varying hierarchical levels of power, you have access to a diverse set of perspectives and insight. Consider meeting with each person from your management team in ascending order to gain insight into the paths they've taken. Perspective is always good when making career decisions. Additionally, ask them questions about how you can identify your career track and what they recommend for you.

Your mentors are your coaches. Leverage them to help you identify your career track. Share your interests and your passions with your mentors and ask them to help you identify a career track that would align with your desires. Also, ask them questions about the available career tracks, as well as the benefits and downfalls of each one. Remember, your mentor is someone with whom you can be transparent, so be frank in your informal discussions and really pick their brain.

Your sponsors are your cheerleaders. They want to endorse you for opportunities, and if they have a greater understanding of your interests, then they can help you get there. Remember, your sponsor is someone in a leadership position within your company, so he or she possesses a greater understanding of career navigation and of the company as a whole. Meet with your sponsors to learn how they've each steered their career and ask them ways in which you can identify your career track. Once you establish your career track, share this information with your sponsors, so they can begin to endorse you for opportunities that will help develop and mature your skills and talents.

Determining Your Career Track

You are not expected to know your exact career track upon starting with the company. In fact, most recent college graduates and even young professionals have a vast range of interests in the beginning. However, exposure to various different organizations within the company and working with cross-functional teams will help narrow down your interests.

The first eighteen months of working in your company will be focused on the strategies outlined in Parts I and II of this book. Your development during this time is a general applicable foundation for most career tracks. After approximately three years of working at the company, you should have sufficient exposure to discuss a career track that satisfies your interests and desires. Deciding upon a career track will help focus your pursuit of opportunities and exposure that you need for your development. Note, at any time in your career, you can choose to change your career track to accommodate newly found interests, adjust to the changes within your life's direction, or better support your work-life balance.

How I Discovered My Career Track

At work, I supported a number of different programs and initiatives, and for some reason, I always admired the role of the program manager. Based on my observations, the program manager set the vision and the tone for the overall development and execution of the program. The program manager also interfaced with every aspect of the program, from client-facing to negotiations, program deliverables to the client, status updates to executive management, daily encounters with the leads of every aspect of the program, and overarching communication to all staff. This person possessed a high level of understanding of the program from cradle to grave. There was something about this role that intrigued me, and I developed the desire to pursue a career track for program management.

You do not need to limit yourself to a career track. A career track is simply a guide to help you think about the skills and experiences that are recommended for you to evolve into a desired position within the company. There are no straight lines in becoming who you aspire to be within the corporate hierarchy, so use a career track as a guide and not as a requirement.

It's possible to pursue more than one career track. As you grow and gain more experience while investing years of service in Corporate America, you will discover the most suitable career track for you. But for now, pursue the track(s) that match your interests and share a fundamental commonality, if possible. Also, if you choose a career track that later doesn't satisfy your heart's desires, then you can change it. After identifying a career track, you should create a development plan.

Career Tracks Are Subject to Change

Career tracks can vary from company to company, but in many cases, the foundation of experiences and skills for the desired role likely still hold true. Also, experiences can influence you to change your career track. This is because exposure will either pique or redirect your interest. Both can be beneficial and valuable to your development. Regardless, an experience can change your path forward. It's okay to change your career track as you discover your gifts and talents. As a matter of fact, many people change their career track as they evolve within their professional development and progress outside of work in their personal lives.

Nefisms

- Career tracks offer optional growth potential.
- Career tracks inspire career evolution.
- Career tracks model strategic alignment to company structure.
- Exposure can influence a change in a career track.
- Passion can lead you along a new career track.

10

___

Create a Development Plan

A development plan is a guided strategy that helps you reach an intended goal. It maps out the steps that will lead you towards your goal, which is critical for success. The steps in the development plan consist of skills, experience, and training that are needed to help you successfully accomplish each step—it's really that simple. The development plan essentially supports your career track by establishing actionable goals to help you get there.

Without a vision, how do you know where you're going? Consider creating a development plan to help establish the strategy for your career. When you develop a strategy by way of a development plan, you create a vision for your career. Further, a development plan is useful because it's an executable path forward towards an objective. It is literally going to help you win! Additionally, it's beneficial because it's a resource that can facilitate new experiences and exposure—now that's what I consider playing it to win.

How to Create a Development Plan

First, determine what you want to evolve towards. Based on your aspiration, you should develop a short- or long-term development plan as appropriate. I recommend creating a 1-3-5-7-year development plan. Set a goal for where you want to be in your career in seven years. Then meet with your mentors to help you develop realistic milestones at one, three, and five-year benchmarks that will lead to the achievement of your seven-year goal. With your mentors, identify the skills, experience, and training courses that will be required for you to accomplish each benchmark along the way to your ultimate goals. After completing this exercise with your mentors, share your drafted development plan with your manager to review and endorse.

How I Created My Development Plan

Once I realized that I wanted to become a program manager, I met with my mentor to discuss my career interest. After meeting with him, he asked me to draft a sample document outlining the milestones of roles I would need to perform to help qualify me for the role of a program manager. So I leveraged my exposure to programs I supported, as well as internal career path resources, to draft the document. Two weeks later, I met with my mentor. He reviewed my draft and suggested incorporating available training opportunities and experiences to support me in each milestone role and prepare me for the next milestone. After this revision, he reviewed it again for accuracy. He then asked me to share the final draft with my manager for buy-in to begin helping me find opportunities to support my development plan.

A development plan is structured with milestones and tasks. When you're drafting your plan, build upon content found in your desired career track to indicate milestones. Next, incorporate your mentor's insights to compose a series of tasks that will help you reach each milestone. A diverse set of job experiences, leadership development, training opportunities, and exposure contribute to the ingredients. Your mentors and your manager will be valuable in helping you create your development plan.

I Have a Development Plan—Now What?

Once you have agreed upon a development plan with your manager, begin to seek opportunities that will help you gain the skills and experience needed to support your plan. This is where you truly leverage your team. Discuss with your manager, mentors, and sponsors what skills and experience you are currently seeking to obtain. Ask your team what short-term and long-term opportunities currently exist or will soon become available for you. Share your development plan with your team. Why? Because these are the people you have identified who want to see you win. They are your cheerleaders and coaches, so you have to sustain open lines of communication with them.

Actively seek opportunities on your own to develop your skills and experience. Explore current and upcoming training opportunities that can help develop and mature your skill set. Also, leverage your interdisciplinary network, which we'll discuss more in Strategy 13, to gain an awareness of existing or upcoming opportunities and to socialize your interests and current skill set.

Additionally, review your development plan quarterly to ensure that you're completing your identified tasks and striving towards your milestones. At this frequency, it helps keep you focused and aligned with your long-term desires. Further, at the end of each year, review what you have accomplished within your development plan and make any necessary updates or adjustments with the guidance of your mentors and manager.

Training Opportunities

Training opportunities help you to build your skills, so take advantage of them! There are usually a vast number of training courses that are available to you at your company and through external entities. Identify which courses are of interest to you and support your development. Then discuss them with your manager. Your manager typically has to approve your training hours, so show him or her how this training course supports your development and how it's relevant to any current or upcoming projects in which you are or will be involved.

My Approach to Training Opportunities for Development

I seek training opportunities that directly support my development plan or the functionality of my current role on a program. Each of the milestone roles found within my development plan has associated training dependencies, and I find available training opportunities via my company's internal learning and development platform to help check those boxes off my plan.

On-the-Job Training?

On-the-job training is a form of internal development of your skills by way of supporting an organizational effort. With on-the-job training, you learn how to approach and solve real-time problems and issues. It typically entails being paired with an individual who is skilled in that specific area and who has the capacity to guide your learning and development process as it relates to the problem at hand. This approach is a highly effective way to learn within the workplace.

On-the-job training also offers you an opportunity to learn how your company approaches and solves problems. In fact, it can arguably be the best way to learn. The opportunity to work side-by-side with an organization's subject matter expert will help you learn and develop the tactics to develop a solution for the problem domain. This is beneficial for you because it allows you to learn from the best.

Through on-the-job training, you can be inquisitive and ask meaningful and complex questions of a subject matter expert. You can learn tips, tricks, and best practices that you wouldn't be able to discover on your own at a rapid pace. Getting your questions answered instantaneously will help expedite your learning experience and develop your skills at a higher rate.

My Approach to On-the-Job Training for Development

When an opportunity for on-the-job training presented itself, I took full advantage of it: whether it was learning how to properly run a program status meeting, develop models within a new software tool, correctly write system requirements, write technical documents and executive briefings, establish customer relationships, etc. Every time a learning opportunity was available, I viewed it as a growth opportunity to develop or mature my current skills with the mindset of supporting my development as a program manager. Therefore, when engaging in on-the-job training, I asked lots of questions and always ensured I gained an understanding of the exemplified approach and why it was executed that way.

Stretch Assignments

Don't be afraid of opportunities that are difficult, complex, or outside your comfort zone. Many refer to such opportunities as stretch assignments. Stretch assignments are opportunities that require you to develop and diversify your skills and knowledge. Through a stretch assignment, you will develop the tenacity to face and overcome barriers and obstacles that will shape your character for the person you will become in your career. Stretch assignments can help advance your development.

My Approach to Stretch Assignments

I've learned that stretch assignments are opportunities to convert your potential into tangible skills and experience. One Friday morning, I was called into a meeting and asked to become a manager for eight staff members. As a senior engineer and a technically focused employee with zero direct reports, I never had any interest in managing people from a functional perspective. So when this opportunity presented itself to me, I wasn't a bit excited, but I stepped into the role with an optimistic perspective and the willingness to stretch beyond my comfort zone. The first few weeks were quite overwhelming and chaotic, but I quickly adapted to the demands of the role. It required me to arrive at the office two hours earlier than usual and become flexible with my time throughout the day to accommodate the needs of staff in parallel to my technical engineering responsibilities. As time progressed, I quickly evolved into a great manager, and one of my direct reports awarded me with the Passionate Service Award for my function as a career manager. Needless to say, this particular stretch assignment drew out a greater version of myself and a new passion for managing people, which ultimately converted the potential that my leadership recognized in me into a tangible new skill.

Development Plans Are Subject to Change

Like many things in life, a development plan can change, similar to how your career track can change. For example, a development plan can change if you leave your company. Although you may leave a particular company, the basis of your development towards your desired ultimate goal should still hold true—for the most part. Additionally, new experiences or exposure can influence you to modify your development plan, and this can be a good thing. Why? Because it's okay to change your development plan in an effort to better align to the discovery of your true gifts and talents.

Why I Modified My Development Plan

After my stretch assignment as a manager, I realized that I enjoyed managing people. Now I'm interested in opportunities that will allow me to manage staff in various capacities. This interest does not drastically change my development plan, but I simply modified it for better agility in my performance and execution.

Nefisms

- Development plans provide a roadmap for success.
- Development plans trace your progression.
- Development plans actualize the vision for your career.
- Personal interests contribute to a customized development plan.
- Opportunities realize your evolution along a development plan.

11

Seek New Opportunities

Seeking new opportunities is critical to support your development plan. Without opportunities, there is no platform for you to exercise your potential for the next level. Opportunities are vehicles to develop and prepare you for the next coming attraction of your career, as well as a platform to display your contribution and value to your customer, stakeholder, management, or leadership.

How to Find Opportunities

Opportunities can always be found in any organization or company. Problems and needs are considered opportunities, so be able to recognize that opportunities are birthed out of need or conflict, and position yourself to offer your skills and talents to contribute to the solution.

Your manager, mentors, and sponsors are great resources to help you identify opportunities. They have insight into organizational needs and problems that you may not necessarily be able to access at your level in the hierarchy. They also serve to recommend and endorse you for new opportunities that support your growth and development plan, which will require you to always be willing to learn new things.

Types of opportunities to seek:

- Seek opportunities to apply your knowledge to new and different applications.
- Seek opportunities to expand your breadth of knowledge.

Opportunities that require you to apply your knowledge to new and different applications are great prospects to mature your skill set. By diversifying the application, you will discover new ways of approaching the same type of problem, but in a different way. This will grow the depth of your knowledge and differentiate your skill set, which will lend itself to helping you become a person of increased value.

Opportunities that expand your breadth of knowledge as you continue to build depth within your subject area will position you for continual, progressive success. As you develop your subject matter expertise, gain knowledge in lateral domains that support your subject matter area. Your ability to assess a problem, especially a complex one, and execute a solution can require an understanding of the dependencies driving the root cause. In this case, how your breadth of knowledge crosses into other domains will influence the degree to which you can solve the problem. The more complex the problems you can solve, the greater your value to the organization and the company.

My Approach to Finding New Opportunities

Over time, I have gained an understanding that problems create opportunity. Therefore, whenever I stumble upon someone with a problem, an issue, or concern, I recognize it as a moment to create a new opportunity for growth, development, or service.

I recently participated in a conference call with my senior leadership. During the call, my senior leadership highlighted numerous business development captures that were rapidly approaching, and three of them were assigned to my direct leader. I could recognize that he was overwhelmed by the thought of this, so after the call, I offered my help to him. I asked him, "Do you need help with any of the captures? Let me know. I have experience with business development captures, and I'm really good at strategy." He responded, "Okay, I could use your help, but let me think about where I can use you." A few days later, he sent me an initial email with a number of tasks to contribute to the effort, and he later named me his requirements lead for the business development capture. This was a new opportunity for me to function as a requirements lead and a worthwhile experience to learn from my senior leadership and his peers through the process. However, this new opportunity would never have been created unless I'd recognized the need and positioned myself to be a solution through service.

Marketing Yourself for New Opportunities

It's necessary to market yourself for new opportunities. People need to know that you possess the skills, knowledge, and experience to support an effort. Additionally, people in your organization need to know the types of problems that you can solve and the types of solutions you can and have delivered in the past. Find and explore platforms within your organization and company that will allow you to showcase and strategically market yourself as a solution for particular types of problems the business is facing.

How I Market Myself for New Opportunities

Similar to how I find new opportunities, I market myself in the office by offering to help others complete their tasks. I've found that this is the best way to seamlessly showcase my skills, knowledge, and understanding in the most practical way.

Previously, one of the leads on a program I supported was burdened by a challenging task that minimized his time to address another task for the program management office (PMO). I recognized what was needed, and I offered my time to help move this outstanding task forward. As I began working on this task at the PMO level, I was able to join weekly status calls with the PMO that allowed me to market my skills, knowledge, and work effort at the highest level of the program. In return, I was later offered new opportunities at the program management level.

Never Get Comfortable in an Opportunity

When you are no longer being challenged in your position, it is either an indication that you have mastered your role and responsibilities, or there are no new opportunities for growth and development. It also suggests that you are now comfortable. When you become comfortable, it is a signal that your skills are dormant, and you are likely not growing beyond your current capacity. Stagnant growth translates to stagnant salary, stagnant recognition, and stagnant opportunity—all things that you ought to avoid.

Always explore ways to offer additional value to the opportunity for which you're currently providing a solution. There's almost always a way to conduct business more effectively or more efficiently.

How I Continue to Challenge Myself within an Opportunity

I've learned that comfort can create complacency, and where there is comfort, there lies minimal opportunity for growth. With this understanding, I challenge myself with an opportunity each time I find myself in a position of comfort. Typically, when this occurs, I ask others on my team if they need help with anything. Usually, through my offers to help, I discover a number of tasks I can support that generally expand my knowledge base and create a new challenge within my already existing opportunity.

Nefisms

- Opportunities can create elevation.
- Opportunities can expand your territory.
- Opportunities challenge your perception.
- Obstacles can be redefined through new opportunities.
- Growth potential is realized through opportunity.

12

Manage Your Time Effectively

Time management is the ability to appropriately schedule and execute your objectives within a specified time period. I know this can be intimidating, but take a deep breath. Managing time can be a difficult task, but your success greatly depends on it, especially if you seek positions of leadership. You should manage your time because it will evoke a level of discipline that's required to win in the workplace, as well as in life. When you manage your time effectively, you can reap the satisfaction of accomplishment—and the more you accomplish, the more you will want to accomplish.

How to Manage Your Time Effectively

The trick to managing your time effectively is by writing down what you intend to do each day and how much time you expect to spend on each task before you actually start your day. Beginning a new day already knowing what you will achieve and how your time is allocated that day will create a sense of momentum. Throughout the day, remind yourself of your goals for that day to help keep you on track.

My Approach to Effective Time Management

Before the start of every week, I draft a schedule of my time for the week. I outline how I expect to spend my time for personal and professional activities across the coming seven days. In regard to daily professional action items, each evening I write down what I hope to accomplish the next day. When I enter the office each morning, I begin executing those action items according to their level of priority.

Strategies to help manage your time effectively:

a) Set a goal you want to accomplish.

b) Write down your goal and set a date by which you want to achieve it.

c) Create a timeline for how you plan to accomplish your goal.

d) Be disciplined in accomplishing tasks that lead to the achievement of your goal by scheduling time every day to work towards this goal.

Develop Discipline over Your Time

Managing your time effectively requires discipline. Like most things in life, discipline is necessary for success. You must be disciplined to stay focused in striving towards your objective when constrained by time. Discipline will fuel you to become more accountable for the execution of your objectives, which will lend itself to managing your time more effectively—that's really the hidden secret to discipline. You can begin to develop discipline for managing your time effectively by first holding yourself accountable for accomplishing the desired outcome. Then be responsible with your time. I know this can be the most difficult part, but monitoring your distractions and minimizing them will positively influence your focus. Be intentional about placing yourself in an environment that eliminates distractions for you. Additionally, identify an accountability partner, someone who will hold you accountable for the goals you said you would accomplish. This person can also serve as your encourager, thus motivating you to increase your level of discipline.

How I Developed Discipline

The key to developing discipline is rooted within one's level of consistency and self-control. My level of discipline has grown tremendously over the years as a result of my level of commitment. I'm committed to being excellent across every area of my life. Daily, I own my roles and responsibilities and set forth to fulfill and complete each and every task associated with them. I also set a high level of expectation for myself, which helps me develop the level of self-control needed to manifest great discipline. Through consistency and self-control, I've been able to develop high levels of discipline in many areas of my life, including my professional development.

Minimize Distractions

Distractions are people, places, things, events, etc. that negatively disrupt your scheduled time. Try acknowledging when you are presented with a distraction and choose to continue to use your time in the productive manner instead. No matter how big or small, distractions are potential time killers and setbacks that can be avoided. Yes, you can really avoid distractions! You can first minimize distractions by silencing your phone or putting it on airplane mode. Then, find a quiet place where you can focus and concentrate—remember, you need maximum focus if you're going to win in the workplace. Next, before you start your tasks, schedule a time to take a break so you don't get fatigued while concentrating on your tasks. This is important because you need a strategic break to help you refuel and collect your thoughts and ideas. Additionally, incorporate balance and inspiration into your day after accomplishing a task. This is necessary to minimize distractions. It will encourage your mind to move forward in accomplishing a task because it knows that it will receive positive reinforcement afterward.

My Approach to Minimizing Distractions

To help me minimize distractions, I aim to create environments that foster focus. When I need to concentrate on a particular task, I first place my phone on silent. I've found that my cell phone is the number one deterrent to successfully completing many of my tasks. Therefore, this is the first thing I address to help support my focus. Then, I set a time duration for how long I plan to work on that particular task. If I'm home, I'll also light a candle to help relax me, which creates a better environment to concentrate. Next, I start the task at hand for the indicated period of time. This is how I generally minimize distractions.

Balance and Prioritize Work Assignments

The best way to balance your work assignments is by scheduling them on a calendar. In fact, calendars are a secret weapon to help create balance. Discover the deadline for each assignment and then place it on your calendar. A rule of thumb is to begin on the assignment that has the earliest deadline. This approach seems straightforward, but deadlines often overlap. In such case, you must manage your time effectively to establish a rhythm that will help meet your deadlines.

How I Balance Work Assignments

I generally balance work assignments based upon their deadlines and the associated milestones, if applicable, that progress towards the deadline. Similar to how I manage my time, I tend to schedule work assignments in my Microsoft Outlook calendar as meetings to designate time to work on each of the assignments.

The distribution and delegation of work will help you balance your workload. If there are team members who have the bandwidth to assist you in any way, don't be afraid or too shy to ask for help. Success is a collaborative effort that will always necessitate help. Plus, it can become stressful or nearly impossible to meet every deadline allocated to you when you don't have sufficient time. That's why you must be realistic about the level of effort for which you need assistance. Do not ask for help simply because you're lazy. That will not yield in your favor. Instead, it will work against you. Be strategic in your approach and communicate the details of your needs.

How to Prioritize Your Work Assignments

When faced with multiple assignments, ask your manager which assignment he or she would prefer you to attack first. This is important because you will frequently be faced with this instance. Let your manager decide which deliverable is of higher importance to him or her. Do not take on the responsibility of prioritizing tasks unless you already know you can complete all your tasks by the intended due date. Even if you can complete each task by the deadline, you still need to understand your manager's expectations. Additionally, sometimes your manager is so consumed with various tasks that he or she might forget what work they already allocated to you. This is why it's important to make him or her aware of the tasks you are currently working on and ask for direction in prioritization. As we discussed in Strategy 4, it's critical that you establish a trusting and reliable professional relationship with your manager; so inquiring about the prioritization of your work will help mature the relationship.

How I Prioritize My Work Assignments

I tend to prioritize my work assignments based on a number of different factors. The first factor is the scheduled deadline. The next factor is the level of urgency, and the following factor is the level of dependency. However, whenever I need guidance on prioritizing my assignments, I ask my leadership for guidance or negotiate to extend the timeframe for delivery when applicable.

Nefisms

- Time management influences your ability to achieve completion.
- Time management is shaped through discipline.
- Time management challenges procrastination.
- Balance results from adequate time management.
- Prioritization can initialize time management.

13

Create an Interdisciplinary Network

A network is a collection of people who share and exchange thoughts, ideas, and information. An interdisciplinary network is a collection of people with diverse skill sets, disciplines, gifts, and talents. It's a network that is intentionally built for diversity. You should strive to create an interdisciplinary network so you can gain access to information that crosses boundaries beyond your exposure. An interdisciplinary network is different from a regular network because you, the creator of your network, make an intentional effort to connect and establish relationships with knowledgeable people across a vast number of domains and management levels.

Benefits of an Interdisciplinary Network

An interdisciplinary network can offer you a diversity of opportunities that provide depth and breadth of skills and experiences. As you grow and evolve in your career, you want to have a depth and breadth of knowledge and understanding to win in the workplace. This will be a necessary key that differentiates you from your peers and competitors.

An interdisciplinary network will best support your development plan and generate great benefit for you. The first direct benefit of an interdisciplinary network is knowledge. The knowledge from the diversity of your network will help you gain new information and supply a diverse set of perspectives. This interdisciplinary network will benefit your career by offering you a number of approaches that can be leveraged to solve technical problems and devise new approaches. Even more, an interdisciplinary network can benefit your personal development by helping you navigate and overcome a range of obstacles you'll face in the workplace.

How to Build an Interdisciplinary Network

An interdisciplinary network is largely built through exposure. You must be willing to meet and collaborate with people from different fields, disciplines, and organizations. Yes, this requires work. But learning how each discipline and organization is interconnected to solve a problem, and learning the inputs and outputs of each subject area in order to deliver a solution, will help you gain the knowledge and wisdom to lead large-scale efforts and solve complex problems.

How I Built My Interdisciplinary Network

I've found that the best way to build my network is by attending networking events and supporting volunteer activities. I built my interdisciplinary network over time by attending internal networking events across my company. I would have small chats with random folks I didn't know, and when I met someone with shared similarities or interests, I followed up with them after the event with a lunch invitation to build an ongoing professional relationship with them. Additionally, I built most of my interdisciplinary network by supporting company-sponsored volunteer activities. I discovered that the beauty of company-sponsored activities is that they draw together folks from different areas across the company with a shared interest in the mission of the activity. This becomes a melting pot to establish professional relationships with folks who share a common interest with you. This was my strategic approach to building my interdisciplinary network.

Who should be in your interdisciplinary network?

- A minimum of one to two people from each organization of your company.
- Representation from diverse cultural backgrounds.
- Representation from every level of leadership.
- Different genders, etc.
- Varying ages.
- Staff representing various geographical locations.

Strategies to solicit people to be in your interdisciplinary network:

- Attend networking events.
  - Get people business cards and follow up with people via email to schedule a meeting.
- Have information sessions.
  - Schedule an information session with someone you admire in the workplace.
- Have lunch with someone on your team.
- Be social!
  - Converse with people when you enter a room.

When building an interdisciplinary network, there is no limit on the number of people you can have within your network. However, you want to ensure that you're feeding the relationships that you establish because you never want to contact someone only when you need them. This is never a good thing or position to be in, especially when you truly need their help. So strive to build a network that you can strategically manage. Further, in today's world, we are more connected than ever before, with social media and vast online platforms, so there are few challenges to building an interdisciplinary network.

Expand Your Interdisciplinary Network

Once you've built your interdisciplinary network within your company, it's time to expand to those outside of your company.

Strategies to expand your interdisciplinary network:

- Attend networking events.
- Join new social circles and organizations.
- Volunteer to support activities that align with your new interests.

In addition to these strategies, leverage your existing network to help you expand your interdisciplinary network. Ask individuals if they can recommend someone who has expertise in a particular area in which you're seeking information. As you expand your network, remember to continue to feed the relationships that you've established.

How I Continue to Expand My Interdisciplinary Network

I've found that it's valuable to develop a network outside my internal company. I never know when I may need an outside opinion, different perspective to help me make good career decisions, or additional opportunities external to my company. I value my internal company network, but I also cherish my external network. I built my external interdisciplinary network much in the same way I built my internal interdisciplinary network—by attending networking functions and participating in volunteer activities. As a local to the Washington, DC Metro area, I consistently attend networking functions for young professionals throughout the region. I've found that it's a great way to meet young professionals from multiple industries and domains. As a professional woman in engineering and an alumna of the University of Maryland, College Park, I volunteer my time and gifts daily in support of STEM outreach activities that mentor and empower young women. You see, I rely on my interests and passions to support my actions when seeking to expand my external network.

Nefisms

- A network is an invaluable asset.
- Networking can diversify your resources.
- Networking can extend your level of influence.
- Professional growth is critically dependent upon a supportive network.
- Networking is comprised of proportional deposits and withdrawals.

Part Four

Strategic Development

Develop the character and integrity needed to complement your professional growth.

14

Develop Effective Communication Skills

Your success in the workplace depends largely on your ability to communicate effectively. When you open your mouth, you communicate to the world who you are. Therefore, it is necessary that you develop the skills needed to communicate your thoughts, ideas, and solutions in both verbal and written forms.

Strategies to become an effective communicator:

- Assess your verbal and written communication skills.

- Seek training opportunities to help develop your communication skills.

- Practice and improve your verbal communication skills through training and giving presentations.

- Be mindful of your non-verbal communication and pay attention to your body language and how you use your hands while engaging with people.

- Practice and develop your written communication skills by writing memos, white papers, technical articles, and publications.

The first step to becoming an effective communicator is evaluating where you currently stand. Assess your verbal communication skills. How do you speak? What level of vocabulary do you use to express yourself? Do you speak clearly? Do you enunciate when you speak? Then assess your written communication skills. How do you compose emails? How do you currently compose technical reports? What level of vocabulary do you use in your writing? How do you organize your thoughts on paper? Do your thoughts flow logically? Do the readers clearly understand the point you're trying to make? We generally have an understanding of what areas within our verbal and written communication need improvement. However, if you're unsure, then I encourage you to solicit feedback.

Seek training opportunities to help develop your communication skills. There exist numerous training courses online that can help you become an effective communicator. Additionally, there are countless books that can help you build your communication skills as well. Your company may also offer training opportunities for you to improve your overall verbal and written communication skills. I highly suggest that you seek these internal training opportunities within your company before exploring external opportunities. Demonstrating your interest to grow your communications skills will gain you notice from your management team. This is because you're taking the initiative to develop the skill set needed to improve your performance and lead effectively.

Verbal Communication

Verbal communication is arguably the most critical form of communication in the workplace. This is because people in the workplace inherently judge you based on your ability to speak. Until this moment, you may have thought speaking is simply opening your mouth and talking. Wrong! There's a socially acceptable workplace style of speech, and you must learn it if you want to advance within your organization and company.

Toastmasters is a good platform to help you develop your verbal communication skills. There, you practice speaking skills through a variety of exercises. Toastmasters will assist you in honing your presentation skills, which will increase your level of confidence and speech awareness when communicating verbally with others. Some companies offer Toastmasters or a generic version of it within the organization. Explore your company's offerings before exploring external Toastmaster classes.

How I Developed My Verbal Communication Skills

For two years, I intentionally spent time building my communication skills. I had a limited vocabulary and poor enunciation, so I felt intimidated in most professional conversations because of my limitations. However, one day I made a decision to improve. My sister told me that reading books could increase my vocabulary, so despite my lack of desire to read, I started reading one book a month. As I read the books, I started incorporating new vocabulary into my conversations, and as time went on, I increased my toolbox of vocabulary that I could use to better express my thoughts and ideas.

As I spent time reading books, I also focused on better enunciating the words I was reading. I would practice my enunciation while I was at home reading and testing my pronunciation of words throughout candid conversations. Further, I was always open to correction of my pronunciation, which assisted me in my growth. Over time, I would step outside of my comfort zone to take advantage of opportunities to speak in front of others. I strategically used these opportunities to test the growth of my vocabulary and enunciation while developing the clarity and tone of my voice and speech. As time went by, I continuously focused on developing my verbal communication skills. I now have complete confidence during conversations and public speaking.

As you develop your verbal communication skills, be mindful of your non-verbal communication. Non-verbal communication refers to your body language and facial expressions. It's important that you pay attention to your body language and how you use your hands while engaging with people. Your facial expressions are also important when listening and speaking to people. Your non-verbal communication skills can strengthen or weaken your verbal communication. Be mindful of your subtle non-verbal communication habits.

I believe that how you speak is a collection of your tone and personality, clarity and enunciation, and most importantly your vocabulary.

Strategic focus areas for increasing your verbal communication:

- Tone and personality
- Clarity and enunciation
- Vocabulary

The tone you use when speaking shapes the delivery of your content. It largely influences how the listener will receive your information. Expressing your personality through your communication will affect how the listener feels when they receive your information. A strategic combination of tone and personality tailored to the type of information you are delivering will help you shape the impact your communication will have.

Being able to speak clearly will minimize the probability of confusion. When you speak, aim for your listener to understand the content of your thoughts and ideas. Limitations in your ability to fully articulate your thoughts and ideas clearly will prohibit the listener's ability to comprehend you and your intent. Next, any inability to enunciate properly will reduce your perceived level of competency to the listener. Therefore, focus on appropriately enunciating your words when you speak. Note, the listener is listening to the delivery of your content as well as the content itself.

The vocabulary you choose when speaking generally communicates your overall level of competency. Your choice of words can increase the effectiveness of your communication. People in the workplace want to feel enlightened by the delivery of your content and the exchange of your information. So using appropriate vocabulary can create a space of enlightenment, especially when paired with tone, personality, clarity, and enunciation. Therefore, strive to increase and expand your vocabulary—a great way is by reading books.

Written Communication

Written communication conveys your level of intellect and effectiveness through words. Written communication is just as important as verbal communication. That's why it's essential to build your writing skills as you develop your speaking skills.

Becoming an effective written communicator requires practice by writing memos, white papers, technical articles, and publications. You likely won't be great in the beginning, but practice makes perfect. Start by developing your vocabulary by reading books. Then review technical writing to gain insight into how various authors structure their thoughts and ideas. Afterward, practice what you've learned and observed. Put it to practice! It's the only way you're going to grow your writing skills.

How I Developed My Written Communication Skills

Similar to my verbal communication, I struggled with my written communication skills. For as long as I could remember, I was never a good writer. I even feared it. It was so difficult for me to structure my thoughts and ideas on paper, especially considering my limited vocabulary. Having to write my master's thesis is what forced me to step outside of my comfort zone to develop this much-needed skill. After completing my thesis, I submitted a white paper for publication, and it was accepted by an engineering conference. This is what encouraged me to continue to develop my writing skills.

At work, I realized that there was a difference between writing skills for technical deliverables and writing skills for emails. In fact, I discovered that writing skills for emails are just as important as technical writing, if not more. When I first started at the company, I wasn't the best at writing emails. For some reason, I was always cautious of everything I wrote, and I spent considerable time rereading what I wrote before I sent it. However, one day I started observing how others wrote emails and how they expressed their direction and opinions. Over time, I started incorporating similar email structures and word choices into the emails I drafted until I fashioned an approach that still works for me today.

Strategic focus areas for increasing your written communication:

- Emails
- Technical writing
- Vocabulary

Emails are a primary source of communication within the workplace. Your written communication via email can lead to your success or failure. Therefore, having email etiquette can play to your advantage.

Technical writing communicates your expertise in an area or on a specific topic. Technical writing translates your domain knowledge into a structured format that can be published and later consumed by readers within your field of study.

Similar to verbal communication, your choice of vocabulary when composing documents is consequential. It can illustrate your competency in the topic at hand, or it can reduce the perception of your intellect on the topic. With written communication, you must take heed of grammar. Be aware of how you conjugate your verbs, use phrases and prepositions, etc.

Nefisms

- Effective communication skills can impact your growth potential.
- Effective communication skills express who you are.
- Effective communication skills exhibit your level of confidence.
- Intentionality can be expressed through effective communication skills.
- Conflict can be mitigated through effective communication skills.

15

Character Development

Character is a profile description of the qualities and attributes that you possess and exude. Your character usually precedes your presence and validates your actions. Your character is developed through your values, beliefs, and perspectives on life. Your character can evolve by way of life experiences and through the transformation of your mind.

Character development is a gradual process. You must consistently seek ways to become a better human being, and life will present opportunities for you to grow and progress. You will also find that your character shapes the people and resources that are attracted to you, especially in the workplace. As you develop your character, you will adjust the world around you, including your organization at work.

My Approach to Developing My Character

When I think about character development, I imagine the best version of myself—a woman who is kind, patient, loving, sympathetic, trustworthy, responsible, and confident. Then, I evaluate my current attributes against that image. Next, through intentionality, I focus on ways to develop my current attributes to fit this ultimate character of who I want to become. I am proud to exercise these desired characteristics each day.

Strategies to develop your character:

- Assess your character through introspection.
- Identify your strengths and weaknesses.
- Ask your trusted confidants what areas of your character you could improve upon.
- Set goals for the areas you want to develop.
- Be intentional about working on yourself every day.
- Be patient—character development takes time. You won't see results overnight.

The first step in character development is assessing your character through introspection. It's imperative that you take time to evaluate your current values and principles because they largely shape your character. Introspection is an internal process that requires you to be transparent with yourself and who you currently are.

A critical aspect of introspection is identifying your strengths and weaknesses. This process requires being fully honest with yourself to point out what you do well and what you don't do well. Identifying your strengths will help you strategically leverage them on a frequent basis. Identifying your weaknesses will help you build awareness of your deficiencies, such that they do not limit your strengths.

After completing your introspection, ask your trusted confidants what areas of your character you could improve upon. Many times, those exposed to us on a regular basis can recognize our attributes and personality traits that we don't. That's why it's important to seek feedback from confidants to help identify blind spots that your introspection may not reveal.

Character development, like many other areas of development, requires you to set goals for the areas you want to develop. After looking within and seeking feedback from trusted friends, you can determine the areas of opportunity for character development. Set goals for these development opportunities and hold yourself accountable for growth in each area.

Character development requires intentionality, so you have to be mindful about working on yourself every day.

Work on becoming one step better in each area of improvement. Tackle each area in a meaningful way such that people will take notice of your evolution. Intentionality and discipline are the only ways you're going to reach your goals for character development.

Character development takes time. Therefore, you must be patient as you strive to meet your goals. You won't see results overnight. However, don't let the process discourage you. Simply prepare for the evolution and realize that you're working towards a better version of yourself.

Become Someone People Like Working With

Your character in the workplace will largely influence how people interact with you and the capacity at which people are willing to work with you. Most people in the workplace want to collaborate and team up with people they enjoy. At times, this is independent of the individual's skill set and knowledge. However, in some cases, people are willing to overlook inadequate skills and knowledge in lieu of working with someone who possesses the needed skills and knowledge but can deter the team morale. Strive to become a high performer, as discussed in Strategy 1, while simultaneously developing a likeability factor. As a result, people in the workplace will want to work with you because you are a high performer and can also positively contribute to the team morale.

Nefisms

- Character development is an evolution.
- Character development unmasks authenticity.
- Character development contributes to professional and personal growth.
- Opportunities can manifest as a result of character development.
- Opposition can be managed through character development.

16

Leadership Development

Leadership is a position of serving others. Most people would argue that leadership is a position of power and influence, and that's also correct. However, it's the leader's ability to exercise their appointed power and influence to serve others that contributes to effective leadership.

Leadership development begins with you. Take time to discover your strengths and weaknesses. You must be aware of your strengths so you can leverage them to influence the people you lead while acknowledging your weaknesses so they do not hinder your ability to lead.

Leadership development is a journey and a continuous pursuit of your evolution, largely based on your character, self-awareness, and ability to grow your understanding of people.

How I Developed My Leadership Skills

I first started developing my leadership skills in college. I joined professional societies on campus and took on various leadership positions. These campus-level experiences gave me a platform to serve others and to create a level of passion in leadership roles. Through college, I also participated in various professional development activities that built my awareness of leadership. When I started working at a company after college graduation, I immediately sought out leadership roles for volunteer groups and organizations within the company. These platforms helped me build upon my evolving leadership skills. The demonstration of my growing leadership skills led to an opportunity for me to join one of the company's leadership programs. My participation in this program exposed me to different leadership styles, the qualities of an effective leader, and it helped me to explore my strengths and growth opportunities as a leader. This program equipped me with the knowledge and tools that have truly launched me as a leader.

Strategies to develop your leadership characteristics:

- Participate in a leadership development program within your company.
- Serve in a leadership role in a volunteer organization within your company.
- Join a leadership development forum within your company.
- Learn about leadership styles and read books on leadership development.

Participation in a leadership development program within your company is a great way to develop your leadership characteristics. Leadership development programs typically help you explore leadership styles and you evaluate and build your current leadership skills through a variety of exercises. They also help you gain insight into how the company itself views leaders and what they expect from leadership across their organizations.

Serving in a leadership role for a volunteer organization within your company is a wonderful way to build your leadership characteristics while growing your network. Volunteer organizations are generally open to people at any level of the organization who are willing to take on leadership positions. In fact, many organizations desperately need leaders. Therefore, use this volunteer platform to develop and grow your leadership styles and characteristics. This volunteer organization would be a great avenue for trial and error in applying what you currently know about leadership.

Likewise, joining a leadership development forum within your company is a strategic way to network with leaders within the organization and learn about current topics on leadership. Leadership development forums are typically composed of a community of employees interested in leadership at any level within the organization. Many of the employees within the forum typically already hold a leadership position, technical or managerial, within the company and are seeking to increase exposure to go to the next level, mentor others, or simply network. As a Millennial starting in Corporate America, this is a community you want to join to connect with the right people who will help you develop your leadership characteristics through opportunities and mentorship.

The most direct way to learn about leadership styles and characteristics is by reading books. There exist countless books on topics related to leadership development. Find a book that is of interest to you. You can even ask your manager, mentor, or sponsors if they can recommend a leadership book for you to read. This is also a strategic move because you're demonstrating through your actions your initiative to seek new information while sharing your interest in growing your leadership potential and abilities.

Nefisms

- Leadership development is a lifestyle.
- Leadership development is continuous.
- Leadership development is rooted in personal development.
- Leadership is a position of serving others.
- Influence is a fruit of leadership development.

17

Become a Person of Value

A person of value is an individual who possesses a marketable skill set and knowledge that serve the needs and demands of an organization. A person of value also possesses the experiences and lessons learned of how to approach problems, overcome barriers, and deliver solutions for critical areas of demand within the company. Becoming a person of value entails identifying your area of subject matter expertise, seeking out opportunities to grow your skill set, and pivoting to new opportunities to grow your level of value.

How to Become a Person of Value

To become a person of value, you must first identify the critical needs within your industry, domain, company, or organization. Once you identify the needs, explore which area of opportunity is of most interest to you. Then, begin to research the area of opportunity in depth to discover what's already been done, the issues and concerns, who the key players are, and the strategic roadmap.

After becoming knowledgeable of the opportunity space, assess your current skills, knowledge, and experience against the needed skills, knowledge, and experience desired for the space. Identify the gaps that exist and begin to seek opportunities that will help you fill those gaps. This process may require that you move beyond your comfort zone, but it is outside of your comfort zone where you grow and evolve into a person of value.

How I Grew into a Person of Value

I became a person of growing value by focusing and maturing my knowledge in the domain of systems engineering with a concentration on model-based systems engineering (MBSE). I intentionally studied this area from both an academic and industry perspective by performing intensive research within the domain and submitting white papers, journal articles, and conference presentations. Over time, I exercised my growing domain knowledge to support capturing new business, filling knowledge gaps within the company, and developing processes for MBSE across the systems engineering organization.

In parallel to growing my technical domain knowledge and experiences, I was developing business development skills, advancing my leadership skills, and increasing my interpersonal skills. The sum of these developing skills, complemented by my rising technical proficiency, positioned me as a person of value.

Strategies to help you become a person of value:

- Find your niche.
- Study and learn the industry of your niche.
- Learn from the leaders driving and influencing the niche space.
- Become a subject matter expert within your niche.
- Present and brief information about your niche space; this will help you gain exposure.
- Publish content in the area of your niche to demonstrate competency and expertise.
- Develop additional skill sets that are marketable for your industry.
- Grow your communication skills—effective communication is needed to influence people.

Start becoming a person of value by finding your niche. Your niche is an area that highly piques your interest. Generally, it takes time to identify your niche by exploring opportunities to discover your likes and dislikes. When you stumble upon an opportunity that you like, assess your level of passion for it. When you discover that you're passionate about a domain or subject area, perhaps you've now discovered your niche.

Once you've discovered your niche, study and learn the industry of your niche space. Research it through online platforms, publications, and books. Learn about current trends within the space and identify the skills that are needed to succeed there.

Learn from the leaders driving and influencing your niche space. This can be done first by identifying the leaders within your organization and company. Conduct an information session with each leader to seek their views on the niche space and offer your time and services to contribute to the area of the space where they're working. Conferences and forums are also good places to find the leaders driving and influencing your niche space. Participating in external functions outside of your company is great for expanding your niche-network beyond the boundaries of your employer. Learning and exchanging information with a diverse set of leaders within your niche space will position you to acquire data at an enormous rate while maximizing your exposure in the process.

Becoming a subject matter expert within your niche space will position you to become a person of value. As a subject matter expert in your field, people will seek your advice and guidance for strategy and implementation. As a result, you will acquire power and influence. Power and influence are attributes of a person of value. As you acquire such attributes and many others, continue to mature your skill set to sustain and grow your levels of power and influence.

Becoming a person of value also necessitates exposure. Therefore, seek opportunities within your organization to verbally present your subject matter expertise. Participate in company-sponsored technical exchanges to brief colleagues on this information. More people need to learn about your skill set and your level of competency on the subject matter to help increase your exposure. This inherently increases your value.

Publish content in the area of your niche to demonstrate competency and expertise. Publication showcases your knowledge and understanding of the subject area. It additionally exhibits your valuable contribution to the community of your subject area. Further, publications help support your pursuit of gaining and growing value within the area of your niche.

Also, develop additional skills that are marketable for your industry. It's important that you complement your subject matter expertise with leadership and management skills. One phase of becoming a person of value depends largely on your subject matter expertise, but your ability to lead efforts and manage people will grow your value to the next level. Next, gaining a breadth of understanding in peripheral domains to your subject matter expertise will further cultivate your growth—in fact, it helps maximize your value.

Lastly, grow your communication skills. Effective communication is needed to influence people, especially those who will contribute to you becoming a person of value. Becoming a subject matter expert without developing your communication skills can limit your value. Therefore, it's imperative that you improve your verbal and written skills as you grow your subject matter expertise in an effort to maximize your value.

Benefits of Becoming a Person of Value

When you become a person of value, you are able to negotiate for benefits that best accommodate your wants and desires while commanding your salary. As a person of value, you acquire a level of influence over your counterparts and individuals in positions of leadership. By guiding and shaping circumstances through your influence, you create desirable opportunities that can allow you to continue to grow and evolve your skills, knowledge, and experiences that increase your value.

My Perspective on Becoming a Person of Value

Out of the many benefits of becoming a person of value—the most valuable aspect, in my opinion—is your ability to influence. I've learned that influence is powerful, and over the years, I've witnessed it firsthand by respected persons in leadership roles. As a growing person of value, I take my level of influence seriously. I strive to positively influence decisions and actions that yield a desirable solution for the business and the overall team. I also use my influence to help support the development of others. For me, this massive benefit is largely why I continue to grow as a person of value.

Demands on Being a Person of Value

Being a person of value makes you a prized commodity. This is a great feeling as an employee, but it also has its burdens. As a high commodity, you are also in high demand. There are problems that exist within the organization that require your specific skill set. Being a valued commodity implies that you are particularly suited to solving specific type of critical problems. As a result of your talent, you will find yourself pulled in many directions, which can potentially cause stress and exhaustion.

How I Manage Being a Person of Value

I've found that being a person of value places a level of demand on my time and talents. As I continue to demonstrate diverse skills and knowledge and a willingness to learn, I'm contacted to engage in numerous activities or help solve cumbersome problems. To manage these efforts, I strive to prioritize assignments to assist as many people as possible, and oftentimes I have to respectfully decline requests. However, I do tend to choose opportunities largely based upon the level of challenge they offer me to grow further or my ability to incorporate the effort seamlessly into my current bandwidth.

How to Sustain Being a Person of Value

You can sustain your position as a person of value by consistently growing your skills, knowledge, and experiences in an area of need within your industry, domain, organization, or company. As you apply your skills and knowledge, people are exposed to your talent and value. Therefore, seek opportunities to keep your skills and knowledge current; always strive to find platforms to exercise new skills and knowledge, as well as those you aim to mature. Most importantly, consistently seek ways to align your skills and knowledge with the business. This will serve you well in your upward professional mobility.

How I Continue to Grow as a Person of Value

I've discovered that sustaining any position within my career or personal life requires a higher level of effort than I needed to initially assume the position. As such, I continue to grow as a person of value by sharpening my current skills and developing complementary ones. I attend training courses to develop new skills. I read forums to stay abreast of industry best practices. I review available lessons learned to learn from the mistakes of others. I enlarge my network to better support my development and direction of growth. Also, I take on new challenges daily. I've learned that taking on new challenges is what truly expands my value and growth potential exponentially.

Nefisms

- Value creates influence.
- Value can be determined by worth.
- Value is undeniable and irreplaceable.
- Demand increases value.
- Perception can impact value.

Epilogue

Your Career Is a Journey

Much like life, your career is a journey, not a destination. It is a sum of experiential learning and growth. This process is driven by iterative learning, application, and calculated risks. With a strategic mindset, your career journey will likely be an adventure worth living that will lead you into a space of gratification and abundance.

Experiential learning is the phase of acquiring new knowledge and skills through exposure in the workplace. While growth is your ability to convert experiential learning into successful execution at the next level. You see, growth is realized through capturing opportunity. Therefore, you must continually seek new opportunities throughout your career that create an avenue for iterative experiential learning and growth to prosper.

The most amazing aspect of your career is that it's yours. You own the decisions you make, when you make them, and how you make them. You are responsible for spearheading your career. This means only you can determine your successes. Therefore, always be strategic and Play It to Win!

Made in the USA
Middletown, DE
14 September 2020

19600191R00111